D0435634

INSIGHT'S
Bible Reading Guide

OLD TESTAMENT

FROM THE BIBLE-TEACHING MINISTRY OF
CHARLES R. SWINDOLL

INSIGHT'S BIBLE READING GUIDE: OLD TESTAMENT

From the Bible-Teaching Ministry of Charles R. Swindoll

Charles R. Swindoll has devoted his life to the clear, practical teaching and application of God's Word and His grace. A pastor at heart, Chuck has served as senior pastor to congregations in Texas, Massachusetts, and California. He currently pastors Stonebriar Community Church in Frisco, Texas, but Chuck's listening audience extends far beyond a local church body. As a leading program in Christian broadcasting, *Insight for Living* airs in major Christian radio markets around the world, reaching people groups in languages they can understand. Chuck's extensive writing ministry has also served the body of Christ worldwide and his leadership as president and now chancellor of Dallas Theological Seminary has helped prepare and equip a new generation for ministry. Chuck and Cynthia, his partner in life and ministry, have four grown children and ten grandchildren.

Published By:
IFL Publishing House
A Division of Insight for Living
Post Office Box 251007
Plano, Texas 75025-1007

Writers: John Adair, Th.M., Ph.D., Dallas Theological Seminary
Terry Boyle, Th.M., Ph.D., Dallas Theological Seminary
Derrick G. Jeter, Th.M., Dallas Theological Seminary
Barb Peil, M.A., Christian Education, Dallas Theological Seminary
Wayne Stiles, Th.M., D.Min., Dallas Theological Seminary
Editor in Chief: Cynthia Swindoll, President, Insight for Living
Executive Vice President: Wayne Stiles, Th.M., D.Min., Dallas Theological Seminary
Theological Editors: John Adair, Th.M., Ph.D., Dallas Theological Seminary
Derrick G. Jeter, Th.M., Dallas Theological Seminary
Content Editor: Amy L. Snedaker, B.A., English, Rhodes College
Copy Editors: Jim Craft, M.A., English, Mississippi College
Kathryn Merritt, M.A., English, Hardin-Simmons University
Project Coordinator, Creative Ministries: Melanie Munnell, M.A., Humanities,
The University of Texas at Dallas
Project Coordinator, Communications: Sarah Magnoni, A.A.S., University of Wisconsin
Proofreader: Paula McCoy, B.A., English, Texas A&M University-Commerce
Cover Designer: Margaret Gulliford, B.A., Graphic Design, Taylor University
Production Artist: Nancy Gustine, B.F.A., Advertising Art, University of North Texas
Cover Image: Waterfalls near Caesarea Philippi/Banias, Israel; image by Wayne Stiles, Th.M., D.Min.,
Dallas Theological Seminary

ISBN: 978-1-57972-906-6
Printed in the United States of America

TABLE OF CONTENTS

A NOTE FROM CHUCK SWINDOLL

The view from the mountaintop is certainly grand.

You know which peak I mean. The emotional high that comes after a God-given victory. The rich feeling associated with a time of nearness to the Lord. The unmatched knowledge that God has delivered you from a grave evil.

There is nothing like standing atop that mountain. If you've spent any time there at all, you know that before long, you'll find yourself in another of life's dark valleys. The reality of sinful people cannot be ignored. Our hearts wander. Our minds drift. Our steps falter.

How can we limit our time in those self-inflicted vales of darkness? I know of no better way than through the prayerful reading of God's Word. As the psalmist says,

> Your word have I treasured in my heart,
> That I may not sin against You. (Psalm 119:11)

We can't keep God's Word in our hearts if we aren't burying our noses in Scripture.

But reading and knowing God's Word takes time. Like any climb out of a valley, it takes commitment and follow-through. And sometimes we need a little nudge—a nudge to open the Bible and an encouragement to read. Then God's Word will find its way into our hearts.

Consider *Insight's Bible Reading Guide: Old Testament* as that nudge to get you going. This book—designed to guide you through reading the Old Testament in a year—comes divided into fifty-two weeks with five Old Testament readings per week.

In addition, we have included short devotional readings that highlight the significance of the passages you will read that week.

"But Chuck," you might object, "have *you* read Leviticus lately?"

Believe me, I know how difficult some sections of the Old Testament can be. But as a Bible-believing and Bible-preaching pastor, I affirm the value of the whole counsel of God. Trust me. Because you'll be learning about your God, your time in His Word will be beneficial. And the devotionals will bring the toughest sections to life for you . . . even Leviticus!

You've scaled the heights with God. And you've crawled through the deepest doldrums. Reading God's Word won't eliminate sin or suffering from your life. But it will prepare you to walk closely with God when you struggle in the midst of those deep valleys. And that's what we all hope for as we live and grow in Christ, isn't it?

As the hymn writer so eloquently penned . . . *just a closer walk with Thee.* You need only to ascend a small hill to get started—open and read.

Chuck Swindoll

Charles R. Swindoll

Keeping to the Way:
Why We Should Read the Bible

Reading the Bible daily has become one of the calling cards of being a "good Christian." Preachers and teachers regularly mark it as a sign of maturity. Believers in the pews often feel guilty when they haven't read their Bibles for a few days . . . or months. There's only one problem: *God's Word never commands us to have a private and personal Bible-reading time*.

Let that sink in a minute.

While the Bible never commands us to have a personal Bible-reading time, God's Word does make numerous commands regarding our knowledge of Scripture. Paul exhorted Timothy to "give attention to the public reading of Scripture, to exhortation and teaching" (1 Timothy 4:13). The Psalms teach us that the righteous person "meditates" on God's law "day and night" (Psalm 1:2), and the psalmist himself made a point to treasure God's Word in his heart (119:11). God clearly wanted His people to hear His Word and commit that Word to memory so they could benefit from it in daily life. But the command for individual believers to read their Bibles on their own is simply not present.

And for good reason.

For most of human history, including during the years that the Bible was being written, God's people had two significant limitations to reading the Bible: ability and access. Most people through history have been illiterate—unable to read. Further, before the printing press was invented around AD 1440, most people had no access to personal copies of the Bible. So, to encourage people to read the Bible on their own would have seemed strange and, well, impossible.

But the few people who had both the ability to read and access to Scripture have, for more than three millennia, made it a point to read it. Recognizing the fundamental importance of God's Word to the lives of God's people, these few read and faithfully shared it with those who could not read for themselves. Only in the last five hundred years or so, with the coming of Gutenberg's press and the persistence of reformers like Martin Luther, have people far and wide gained access to their own copies of God's Word.

In light of that deep and meaningful tradition, Christians today make it a point to encourage reading the Bible. But it isn't simply because of a tradition that we read. Believers throughout history have recognized the practical benefits of reading God's Word. As a result of reading Scripture, God's people grow in several ways:

1. **We Know God:** When we follow through with our commitment to reading the Bible, we come to know God more deeply. We see His character on display in His great deeds and mighty miracles. We see the beauty of His nature as He condescends to reveal Himself to His creation.

2. **We Know Ourselves:** Reading the Bible regularly increases the chances that we will see ourselves the way God sees us. Human beings have fallen and struggle in the morass of sin. But for those of us who believe, God sees us as His holy and beloved children.

3. **We Know Deliverance:** Bible reading also makes us aware of the deep, abiding, and hopeful message of Scripture— God seeks to redeem and re-create His broken creation. Through faith in His Son Jesus alone, we have hope for the future.

4. **We Know How to Live:** Finally, reading the Bible helps us understand how God wants us to live our lives, how we can keep to His way. We can know the three previous items backward and forward, but if God's Word doesn't work itself out in our lives—if that knowledge never moves from our heads to our hearts—then maybe we don't know as much as we think we do.

In the end, the truth of the matter is this: we read the Bible to know Him and be known by Him. We read to humble ourselves. We read to experience deliverance by God from sin and shame. We read to live as His faithful representatives during our time on earth.

Ultimately, we read because we love Him. And because we love Him, we love and obey His Word (Psalm 119:97, 127, 167). When we love and obey His Word, our love for God flourishes and deepens. And as our love for God grows, our passion for His Word increases, which leads again to an ever-deepening love for our Lord.

With such a beautiful cycle before us, what better reason do we need?

How to Use This Book

This book is divided into fifty-two weekly sections. Each week includes five readings, giving you time to reflect on what you've read or catch up on your reading each week if you miss a day here or there. You will also find that each reading includes passages from Psalms or Proverbs, so you'll enjoy reading those two books throughout the year.

Finally, we have included one devotional per week, designed to give you extra insight into one of the passages you'll be reading that week. Use the blank lines on each page to record a few thoughts, if you're inclined.

And most of all, enjoy your time in the Old Testament. It is sure to become one of the richest times of your day.

INSIGHT'S
Bible Reading Guide
OLD TESTAMENT

I long for Your salvation, O LORD,
And Your law is my delight.
— Psalm 119:174

Week 1

Monday: The Uneasy Perfection of Creation
- ☐ *Genesis 1–3*
- ☐ *Psalm 1*

Tuesday: Take Refuge with God in the Face of Wickedness
- ☐ *Genesis 4–8*
- ☐ *Psalm 2*

Wednesday: God Will Punish, Not Destroy, the Wicked
- ☐ *Genesis 9–11*
- ☐ *Psalm 3*

Thursday: God's Care for His Child
- ☐ *Genesis 12–14*
- ☐ *Psalm 4*

Friday: God's Reward for Faith
- ☐ *Genesis 15–17*
- ☐ *Psalm 5*

What I Want to Remember . . .

_____

_____

_____

_____

_____

_____

Only human life—by God's design—possesses the image of God.
—Charles R. Swindoll

Imaging God

Look in a mirror. The image you see looking back at you is not actually you; however, it shares your likeness. It looks like you in identifiable ways.

Such an analogy helps us understand our creation by God. During the creation of human beings, God proclaimed, "Let Us make man in Our image, according to Our likeness" (Genesis 1:26). In other words, when God created humanity, He created a "mirror image" of Himself. But how, exactly, do human beings image their Creator?

It's true that we resemble God in our rationality, in our free will, and in our dominion over creation. However, the context of God's statement in Genesis 1 provides another suggestion: God creates.

Humanity, like God, has the desire and the ability to create. God creates out of nothing. Human beings create out of the materials God gives us. We create constantly. One builds a chair. Another paints a canvas. Still another cooks a ham and cheese omelet for breakfast. Each of these actions involves taking materials that God has provided and creating something new.

In acts of creation great and small, human beings far and wide, Christian or not, bear the image of their Creator.

Week 2

Monday: Fire from Heaven: The End of Sodom and Gomorrah
- ☐ *Genesis 18–20*
- ☐ *Psalm 6*

Tuesday: A Father's Test: Abraham and Isaac
- ☐ *Genesis 21–23*
- ☐ *Psalm 7*

Wednesday: In Search of a Wife for Isaac
- ☐ *Genesis 24–26*
- ☐ *Psalm 8*

Thursday: The High Price of Deception: Jacob Tricks Esau
- ☐ *Genesis 27–29*
- ☐ *Psalm 9*

Friday: The Many Sons of Jacob and More Family Issues
- ☐ *Genesis 30–33*
- ☐ *Psalm 10*

What I Want to Remember . . .

_____

_____

_____

_____

_____

Abraham demonstrated faith by moving into an uncharted course with one guarantee—that God was with him. Come back to the basics—live by faith. Learn from Abraham: God is with you.

—Charles R. Swindoll

The Choices of Faith

A person's life is a string of choices . . . we can see that truth even in the early pages of the Old Testament. The question for each of us has always been: *Will I choose foolishly or will I choose well?*

Abraham did both.

From the dizzying cliffs of faith, Abraham chose to obey God, making one of the most pivotal choices in history: he prepared to sacrifice Isaac. But God saw Abraham's faith and gave him a way out of the test (Genesis 22:1–14).

Turn the page and you see this same great man of faith shrink like a coward and lie to save his own neck (20:1–7). Here, too, God gave Abraham an exit ramp. But he chose deception instead.

Patterns run in families. Abraham's nephew Lot felt a strange draw toward Sodom. If ever a place illustrated the slippery slope of wrong choices, it was this wicked town. Sodom sat on the shore of the Dead Sea, the lowest place on earth—physically, morally, spiritually. When God warned Lot to get out of town, He gave him a way of escape but told him, *Don't look back.* Lot didn't, but his wife did, and she became an immediate object lesson (19:15–26).

The choices you make today could involve private thoughts or public actions. One thing is consistent: along with every temptation, God provides an exit ramp.

Look for it, take it, and don't look back.

Week 3

Monday: Not by Numbers or Arms but the Lord Is Our Defense
- ☐ *Genesis 34–36*
- ☐ *Psalm 11*

Tuesday: Deception Leads to Slavery, but God Is a Sure Helper
- ☐ *Genesis 37–39*
- ☐ *Psalm 12*

Wednesday: How Long, O Lord, Will My Dreams Haunt Me?
- ☐ *Genesis 40–42*
- ☐ *Psalm 13*

Thursday: The Foolishness of the Unfaithful and the Wisdom of the Righteous
- ☐ *Genesis 43–45*
- ☐ *Psalm 14*

Friday: Security Comes Not in Possessions but in Possessing a Righteous Character
- ☐ *Genesis 46–47*
- ☐ *Psalm 15*

What I Want to Remember . . .

_____

_____

_____

_____

When lust suggests a rendezvous, send Jesus Christ as your representative.

—*Charles R. Swindoll*

Resisting Sexual Temptation

Every person who has cast a shadow across the earth, including Jesus, has faced temptation. And every one of us, except Jesus, has yielded to it.

Doubtless, yielding to temptation is much easier than resisting temptation. But for those who yield, the path of life is strewn with the litter of remorse and shame. Their souls grow sick, not from longing to taste forbidden fruit but for having tasted it. If we wish to avoid such soul sickness, we must resist temptation, especially sexual temptation.

When propositioned to slip into the sultry sin of sensuality, Joseph immediately thought of the consequences. Succumbing to such an appeal would have violated trust, damaged his conscience, and defamed the character of God. Joseph could have cuddled lust and enjoyed its warm embrace, but he repeatedly chose to resist in favor of righteousness.

Sexual temptation is never easily discouraged. It will hound us night and day. It is unreasonable and irrational. Not even quoting Bible verses will diminish its appeal. All we can do is what Joseph did: run — flee — escape. Staying anywhere near it might cause us to stumble.

The battle to stay sexually pure is hard-fought, particularly in our sex-saturated culture. But the example of Joseph teaches us that resisting sensual temptation is possible — with God's help, we *can* overcome!

Week 4

Monday: The Death of Jacob . . . the Fullness of Joy
- [ ] *Genesis 48–50*
- [ ] *Psalm 16*

Tuesday: God's Response to the Prayer for Deliverance
- [ ] *Exodus 1–3*
- [ ] *Psalm 17*

Wednesday: God's Promise to Deliver from the Burden
- [ ] *Exodus 4–6*
- [ ] *Psalm 18:1–19*

Thursday: God's Miraculous Preparation to Deliver
- [ ] *Exodus 7–9*
- [ ] *Psalm 18:20–36*

Friday: God Provides Deliverance: Plagues and Passover
- [ ] *Exodus 10–12*
- [ ] *Psalm 18:37–50*

What I Want to Remember . . .

_____

_____

_____

_____

_____

The book of Exodus gives you a picture of deliverance—a way out. God may graciously use an individual, as He used Moses with the Israelites, to help you through and out of that which is controlling you.

—Charles R. Swindoll

Mindful of God's Provision

The Nile River represented the lifeblood of Egypt. Without its vital supply, Egypt would have been a mere desert in North Africa. The river flooded its banks annually, providing the land with rich silt perfect for farming. Because the flood occurred the same time each year, the Nile determined Egypt's calendar. The Egyptians deified the great river, whose spirit they called "Hapi" and whose waters they considered the bloodstream of "Osiris," their god of the underworld.

Therefore, when God turned the Nile to blood in the first plague of the Exodus, He not only wounded the heart of Egyptian sustenance; He revealed the powerlessness of the Egyptian gods.

Over and over in Exodus, God provided both disaster and deliverance to communicate that He—and no other—was the Lord (Exodus 6:7–8; 7:5, 17; 10:2; 14:4, 18; 16:12).

Today's world offers numerous distractions from the true source of our sustenance and success. God never intended the consistent means of our provision to replace our dependence on Him. From the reliability of the seasons, to the food always ready at the market, to the automatic deposits that appear in our accounts, everything we have flows like a great river from God's gracious hand (Nehemiah 2:18; 6:16; James 1:17).

And He can remove it in a moment to remind us it is so.[1]

Week 5

Monday: God's Miraculous Deliverance on the Banks of the Red Sea
- ☐ *Exodus 13–15*
- ☐ *Psalm 19*

Tuesday: The Lord Answers His People in Times of Trouble
- ☐ *Exodus 16–18*
- ☐ *Psalm 20*

Wednesday: The Ten Commandments . . . Guidance from God's Holy Mountain
- ☐ *Exodus 19–21*
- ☐ *Psalm 21*

Thursday: We Will Be Obedient: Affirming God's Covenant
- ☐ *Exodus 22–24*
- ☐ *Psalm 22*

Friday: Overlaid with Gold: Giving the Best for Worship
- ☐ *Exodus 25–27*
- ☐ *Psalm 23*

What I Want to Remember . . .

_____

_____

_____

_____

The crossing of the Red Sea is to the Old Testament what the Resurrection is to the New.

—*Charles R. Swindoll*

The Lord Will Fight for You

With the Egyptians at their backs and the open sea before them, the Israelites were out of options. Without adequate military force to defend themselves against the mighty Egyptian army, God's people had reached a dead end.

And God had led them there.

The Lord had His reasons. Danger and desperation provide opportunity for devotion and dependence. These people needed to see their faith in God for what it was by seeing God for who He was and is.

On the banks of the Red Sea and removed from their comfort zones, the Israelites complained. Their weak faith failed. They bitterly asked Moses why he had brought them out of Egypt in the first place (Exodus 14:11). Moses answered, "The Lord will fight for you while you keep silent" (14:14). God, in His grace, resurrected their hopes as only He could by parting the waters, leading them through, and destroying the Egyptian armies behind them (14:21–30).

God led Israel to that dead end to give them the proper fear and faith He required of His people. And He does the same for us today, leading us to places of desperation, where only He can work, so that our faith in Him might be tested and strengthened.

Week 6

Monday: For Priests: What to Wear and When
- [ ] *Exodus 28–30*
- [ ] *Psalm 24*

Tuesday: The Golden Calf: Failing the Test
- [ ] *Exodus 31–33*
- [ ] *Psalm 25*

Wednesday: Down from the Mountain
- [ ] *Exodus 34–36*
- [ ] *Psalm 26*

Thursday: Tabernacle Furniture
- [ ] *Exodus 37–40*
- [ ] *Psalm 27*

Friday: Procedure Manual
- [ ] *Leviticus 1–3*
- [ ] *Psalm 28*

What I Want to Remember . . .

_____

_____

_____

_____

When the original holy place was established in the tabernacle, a thick veil kept it from general access. The moment Christ died, that veil was torn in two (from top to bottom), giving us instant access into the presence of a holy God. From that moment on, a sinful people could stand before a holy God with access through Christ's blood.

—Charles R. Swindoll

God's Glory among Us

Nothing that God says should be taken lightly. That's the message written all over Exodus in the details about building the tabernacle. That's right: *sweat the small stuff.*

The description of the tabernacle makes up the largest single subject covered in the Bible — in fact, it's one-third of the book of Exodus. God took great pains to describe everything from whom to what, to how many, to how big, to when. Obedience was in the details . . . and for good reason.

The day the tabernacle was completed, God moved into the neighborhood. This portable sanctuary was the center of the community (literally), and God lived in the heart of the building. His "glory" filled the space (Exodus 40:34 – 38).

What does "*God's glory*" mean? Begin with His splendor, His radiant beauty, His fame, His magnificence — His drop-jaw, unapproachable, other-worldly awesomeness.

In building the place where God's glory would live, the Israelites took justifiable care and operated in responsible reverence. They paid attention to the details. They understood, at least in part, that real obedience is measured not only by the attention you give to the job in front of you but also by your attitude in doing it.

Yes, God is glorified when we *sweat* the small stuff.

Week 7

Monday: An Eternal Flame of Holiness Must Burn
- ☐ Leviticus 4–6
- ☐ Psalm 29

Tuesday: Your Mourning Will Turn to Dancing
- ☐ Leviticus 7–9
- ☐ Psalm 30

Wednesday: Only the Holy Are Like the Lord
- ☐ Leviticus 10–12
- ☐ Psalm 31

Thursday: Blessed Are the Holy in Body and Soul
- ☐ Leviticus 13–15
- ☐ Psalm 32

Friday: Holiness Is Available through God's Own Scapegoat
- ☐ Leviticus 16–18
- ☐ Psalm 33

What I Want to Remember . . .

_____

_____

_____

_____

_____

If you, the sinner, wanted to come to God, the Holy One, the only way was through that God-honored detergent—blood.

—Charles R. Swindoll

BEING HOLY LIKE GOD

What comes to mind when you think about God? Whatever thoughts arise, they say more about you than they do about God.

It's fashionable to prefer a predictable god, not one of mystery; a comfortable god, not one who makes us shudder; a holier-than-us god, but not too holy. In short, we want a god like us, only better.

But God is none of these things.

In His unique otherness, our God reveals the beauty of His holiness, by which we see the ugliness of our wretchedness, as He confronts us with a confounding command: "Be holy, for I am holy" (Leviticus 11:44; see also 11:45; 19:2; 20:7).

The book of Leviticus can feel like a speed bump on the biblical highway. But it was in Leviticus that the Israelites learned what it took to live up to their calling as a "kingdom of priests and a holy nation" (Exodus 19:6). They were to imitate the holy character of God. And when they failed, they were to seek forgiveness and sanctification through prescribed laws.

What was true of the Hebrews so long ago is also true of believers in Christ today. We must imitate God's holy character (1 Peter 1:15–16). But how? We can't do it through our own efforts; we must rely on our holy God. Forgiveness and sanctification come through Jesus's blood. Through faith in His death and resurrection, we are cleansed from sin and receive the Holy Spirit who empowers us to live in holiness.

Week 8

Monday: Pursuing Holiness in a Godless World
- ☐ *Leviticus 19–21*
- ☐ *Psalm 34*

Tuesday: Worship and Rest . . . Rescue and Hope
- ☐ *Leviticus 22–24*
- ☐ *Psalm 35*

Wednesday: Looking Forward to Redemption
- ☐ *Leviticus 25–27*
- ☐ *Psalm 36*

Thursday: God Lives Among Us . . . and Protects Us
- ☐ *Numbers 1–3*
- ☐ *Psalm 37:1–22*

Friday: Responsibilities for God's Holy People
- ☐ *Numbers 4–6*
- ☐ *Psalm 37:23–40*

What I Want to Remember . . .

_____

_____

_____

_____

*We can learn a lesson from nature. Periods of rest always follow the
production of a harvest . . . the land must be allowed time to renew
itself. Constant production without restoration depletes resources and, in
fact, diminishes the quality of what is produced.*

—Charles R. Swindoll

Resting in the Truth: God Provides

As God anticipated His people settling in Canaan, He instructed them to work the land. However, every seventh year they were to let the land lie fallow, as God said: "The land shall have a sabbath rest, a sabbath to the LORD" (Leviticus 25:4). This sabbatical year also allowed for the forgiveness of all debts, and the food that grew on its own was to be used to provide for the poor people and the animals.

As the centuries passed, God's people failed to observe the sabbatical year—for 490 years to be exact. So, in 586 BC, God exiled His people for those seventy years of rest they had failed to give the land (2 Chronicles 36:20–21).

Although *they* had worked the land, it was *God* who provided . . . and He required them to stop working so that they could learn this truth. For even while they rested, God promised to provide (Leviticus 25:20–22; Psalm 127:2).

Some principles remain unchanged. Anyone who has ever lost a job or endured true sacrifice in giving to God's work has felt the tension that faith required during the sabbatical year. Faith involves trust, and trust implies risk—at least from our perspective.

The Father longs for us to recognize that He provides *daily* bread, not careers by which we're set for life. God may keep us on the edge of our means, for there our dependence on Him is more often clearly seen.[2]

Week 9

Monday: Preparation to Worship and Serve the Lord
- ☐ *Numbers 7–8*
- ☐ *Psalm 38*

Tuesday: "Kill Me Now": A Leader's Secret Prayer in the Midst of Complaints
- ☐ *Numbers 9–11*
- ☐ *Psalm 39*

Wednesday: Waiting Patiently, or Not, for the Lord
- ☐ *Numbers 12–14*
- ☐ *Psalm 40*

Thursday: The Lord Undermines Rebellion Swiftly
- ☐ *Numbers 15–17*
- ☐ *Psalm 41*

Friday: God Quenches the Thirst of His People
- ☐ *Numbers 18–20*
- ☐ *Psalm 42*

What I Want to Remember . . .

_____

_____

_____

_____

Numbers tells the story of a tragic pilgrimage, where a group of people who knew better did not live better, and they suffered the consequences of a decision they made at a crisis time in their lives.

—Charles R. Swindoll

The Terrifying Grace of God

On the heels of their deliverance from Egypt and upon receiving the law at Mount Sinai, the Israelites again had an opportunity to trust the Lord's guidance. The people of Israel stood in the wilderness of Paran, a desert country south of the Promised Land blanketed with stones and crisscrossed with mountains. In this barren wilderness, God reminded the people of His gracious promise to give them the land of Canaan.

Moses sent out several men to spy out the land, trying to determine, among other things, whether the land was "fat or lean"—whether or not it produced vegetation (Numbers 13:20). The men eventually returned with a cluster of grapes, a visual representation of God's blessing to His people.

However, even with this succulent gift in the midst of the desert—when was the last time the people had even seen grapes?—God's people complained. They feared the inhabitants of the Promised Land and wished they had died in Egypt (13:31–32; 14:2–4).

God's grace often seems terrifying to His people. It can inspire fear when the greatness of His promise so far exceeds our ability to attain it. God's good and gracious gifts test our faith in that they require us to move beyond our own capacity and trust solely in His provision.

Week 10

Monday: Rebuked by a Donkey
- ☐ Numbers 21–23
- ☐ Psalm 43

Tuesday: Israel Seduced by Unrighteousness
- ☐ Numbers 24–26
- ☐ Psalm 44

Wednesday: Joshua to Succeed Moses
- ☐ Numbers 27–29
- ☐ Psalm 45

Thursday: Settling the Land
- ☐ Numbers 30–32
- ☐ Psalm 46

Friday: Establishing the Boundaries of Canaan
- ☐ Numbers 33–36
- ☐ Psalm 47

What I Want to Remember . . .

_____

_____

_____

_____

I would guess that you never anticipated your personal spiritual pilgrimage would be this hard. Neither did the children of Israel. But every step of the way is under God's watchful eye. Allow God to take away the fear of the unknown and replace it with calm, quiet confidence, underscored with trust.

—Charles R. Swindoll

THE DONKEY SPEAKS

It was a strange day when God opened the mouth of a donkey.

But perhaps even stranger was God allowing a manipulative magician and a pagan to speak for Him. Balaam was both.

Balaam looked like a real prophet. He even got messages from God. But Balaam led people away from God for his own financial gain. Balaam loved money more than he loved God or people, so he deceived them. He used the ministry God gave him for his own purpose and pleasure, all the while trying to ride the fence by sounding godly. Rather comically, God rebuked him through a donkey—or as the apostle Peter called it, "a dumb donkey"—that restrained the madness of the prophet (2 Peter 2:16 NET).

Balaam was eloquent. He was convincing, and people listened to him. False teachers will always have a following. They are slick. They have an impressive style. They seem to be providing reliable "spiritual" instruction, but it's all just a show.

Be on your guard whenever you see pride and wherever there is a love of riches and great pretentiousness, even if it is cloaked in what appears to be light.

Wouldn't it be great if God had some way of signaling us to the fact that somebody is not using His Word correctly? God used a dumb donkey to stop Balaam. He can use anything to protect His Word.

Week 11

Monday: Getting Rid of Old Curses and Making Way for
New Blessings
- ☐ *Deuteronomy 1–3*
- ☐ *Psalm 48*

Tuesday: Listen: Where True Treasure Is Found
- ☐ *Deuteronomy 4–6*
- ☐ *Psalm 49*

Wednesday: Remember: The Lord Is God, All Others Are
Cheap Imitations
- ☐ *Deuteronomy 7–9*
- ☐ *Psalm 50*

Thursday: Fear, but Do Not Be Afraid—the Lord Is Merciful
- ☐ *Deuteronomy 10–12*
- ☐ *Psalm 51*

Friday: Free at Last, Free at Last
- ☐ *Deuteronomy 13–15*
- ☐ *Psalm 52*

What I Want to Remember . . .

---

*What does it mean to love God with all your heart and soul and might?
It means He's the basis on which you see everything else. . . . In short,
He's your everything.*

—Charles R. Swindoll

The Riches of Cancelled Debt

What if your credit card company called today and cancelled your debt completely? And then your mortgage company did the same? No strings attached. Wouldn't that be wonderful? Of course, it won't ever happen because in a world whose gold is god, worshiping at the altar of wealth is a reality of modern-day life. But God had a different financial plan for the Hebrews: they were to cancel debts *permanently* every seven years (Deuteronomy 15:1–3). So just how was anyone to prosper under such an arrangement?

The practice of debt cancellation only applied to fellow Hebrews, not to foreigners (15:3). When the nation became established, God said they would "lend to many nations, but . . . not borrow" (15:6). The Lord would pour out His blessings upon the citizens of Israel (15:4, 6), and His blessings would exceed any amount of cancelled debt. The people needed only to trust and obey (15:5).

The principle we can draw from this scenario is simple: motivated out of compassion for the poor and faith toward God, we should practice open-handed generosity (15:7–11). Perhaps this was what Solomon was thinking about when he wrote:

> One man gives freely, yet gains even more;
> another withholds unduly, but comes to poverty.
> (Proverbs 11:24 NIV)

How great it is when our debts are cancelled. But it is greater still to give generously—even to the point of cancelling debts owed to us.

Week 12

Monday: Grateful for God's Redemption and Provision
- ☐ *Deuteronomy 16–18*
- ☐ *Psalm 53*

Tuesday: Provisions for Mercy and Justice
- ☐ *Deuteronomy 19–21*
- ☐ *Psalm 54*

Wednesday: Provisions for Marriage and Morality
- ☐ *Deuteronomy 22–24*
- ☐ *Psalm 55*

Thursday: Choosing to Obey the Lord
- ☐ *Deuteronomy 25–27*
- ☐ *Psalm 56*

Friday: Facing the Warnings of Disobedience
- ☐ *Deuteronomy 28–29*
- ☐ *Psalm 57*

What I Want to Remember . . .

_____

_____

_____

_____

Deuteronomy gives you a permanent record of the consequences of turning against God. If you're on the verge of a very critical decision that would turn you against God, listen to what God is saying. Take Him seriously.

—Charles R. Swindoll

Our Redeemer and Provider

God required the Hebrews to celebrate the Passover and the Feast of Unleavened Bread at the appointed time of *Abib*, a Hebrew word that refers to the time in spring when the grain begins to ripen. The first Passover occurred on the fifteenth day of *Nisan*, which became the first month of the Hebrew calendar.

Because a Hebrew month extends from new moon to new moon — or every twenty-nine and a half days — each year loses eleven days when compared to the solar calendar. And because the sun determines the seasons and controls plant development, the Hebrews had to compensate to make the lunar month of *Nisan* correspond to the month in which *Abib*, or springtime, occurred each year. The Lord gave the Hebrews a plain explanation for why the celebration should coincide with spring: "For in the month of Abib the LORD your God brought you out of Egypt" (Deuteronomy 16:1).

So, about every third year, the Hebrews added an additional month to make up for the difference. If the nation didn't add the extra month, the lunar calendar would cause the date for the Feast of Unleavened Bread to wander through the seasons year by year. Without the additional month, the holiday would preserve its historical value but lose its agricultural connection to the Promised Land.

By keeping the union between the Exodus and the spring, the Hebrews had an annual, tangible reminder that the same God who redeemed them also provided their sustenance each year. This principle has not changed for us as Christians — the same God who saves us for eternity meets our everyday needs in every season (Romans 8:32; Philippians 4:19).[3]

Week 13

Monday: One Leader Passes the Torch to Another
- ☐ *Deuteronomy 30–32*
- ☐ *Psalm 58*

Tuesday: The Final Words of a Great Man
- ☐ *Deuteronomy 33–34*
- ☐ *Psalm 59*

Wednesday: Be Strong and Courageous
- ☐ *Joshua 1–3*
- ☐ *Psalm 60*

Thursday: And the Walls Came Tumbling Down
- ☐ *Joshua 4–6*
- ☐ *Psalm 61*

Friday: Snatching Victory from the Jaws of Defeat
- ☐ *Joshua 7–9*
- ☐ *Psalm 62*

What I Want to Remember . . .

_____

_____

_____

_____

It's impossible to live victoriously for Christ, honoring Him in your work-a-day, play-a-night world, without courage. That's why God's thrice-spoken command to Joshua is as timeless as it is true: "Be strong and courageous!" (Joshua 1:6–9).

—Charles R. Swindoll

An Essential Quality of Leadership

Moses was dead.

Filling the old prophet's shoes would not be easy. As Moses's successor, Joshua planted his feet on the banks of the Jordan River. Only the width of the flowing river stood between his people — God's people — and the Promised Land. Following the Lord's direction would mean leading the Israelites into open conflict with the inhabitants of Canaan — a terrifying prospect.

How could he prevail? The essential quality of Joshua's leadership, the one that allowed him to follow God faithfully, was something impressed upon him several times before he crossed the Jordan: *courage*.

Joshua heard the exhortation to a courageous life no fewer than six times just before crossing into the Promised Land (Deuteronomy 31:6, 7, 23; Joshua 1:6, 7, 9). The Bible doesn't deny Joshua's natural trepidation; it speaks directly to it. To be considered courageous, Joshua had to stand at the precipice of the unknown with fear threatening to overwhelm him . . . and step forward anyway.

As Joshua led the people across the Jordan, he exhibited the essence of courage: he faced the danger around him and the fear within. He acted on God's behalf in spite of those obstacles, becoming not just a worthy successor to Moses but an example of courageous faith for all to follow.

Week 14

Monday: The Day the Sun Stood Still
- ☐ Joshua 10–12
- ☐ Psalm 63

Tuesday: Getting Settled in the Promised Land
- ☐ Joshua 13–15
- ☐ Psalm 64

Wednesday: Dividing the Land among the Brothers
- ☐ Joshua 16–18
- ☐ Psalm 65

Thursday: Cities of Refuge: A Picture of Mercy
- ☐ Joshua 19–21
- ☐ Psalm 66

Friday: Joshua's Farewell Speech
- ☐ Joshua 22–24
- ☐ Psalm 67

What I Want to Remember . . .

_____

_____

_____

_____

You want to be a man or a woman of God? Spend close time with people of God—preferably one or two that you greatly respect. Learn their ways. Learn how it's done. Glean from them the techniques and the character development that have made them great. And then you do it too.

—Charles R. Swindoll

TAKE THAT MOUNTAIN!

Age has nothing to do with your vision.

Caleb was 40 years old when he was sent to spy out Canaan. He was 78 when the Israelites took possession of the land. At age 85, Caleb asked to be sent back into battle to lay claim to another section of land. What a man! Catch his rugged spirit as he said, in effect, "Whatever life throws at me, I'm ready. I'm as strong now as I was forty-five years ago. Let me at 'em!" The last major scene Joshua recorded of 85-year-old Caleb depicts Caleb scaling a mountain, ready to take on giants. He was a man of vision, in spite of his advanced age (Joshua 15:13–19).

Caleb lived through the Exodus from Egypt, through the forty days of spying out the land, through the forty wilderness years, and then he stood on the edge of Canaan again. He and Joshua were the only two adults from the Exodus who survived long enough to live in Canaan. The Lord judged everyone else for their lack of faith. Sure, Caleb saw the giants in the land, too, but they were small compared to his big God.

No matter your age, keep your goals in focus. What is your mountain? Go after it! Like Caleb, keep your sights on God and follow Him *fully*.

Week 15

Monday: A Cycle of Foolishness
- ☐ Judges 1–3
- ☐ Psalm 68:1–19

Tuesday: Wonder Woman: Wife, Judge, and Deliverer
- ☐ Judges 4–5
- ☐ Psalm 68:20–35

Wednesday: A Chicken Who Became a Great Man of Valor
- ☐ Judges 6–8
- ☐ Psalm 69:1–19

Thursday: King of the Trees
- ☐ Judges 9–10
- ☐ Psalm 69:20–36

Friday: A Mighty Warrior and the Birth of the Mightiest Man
- ☐ Judges 11–13
- ☐ Psalm 70

What I Want to Remember . . .

_____

_____

_____

_____

_____

Why in the world did the people of Judges, who had been so victorious under Joshua, fall into failure? Erosion. Erosion is never noisy. Erosion is always silent, unobtrusive, imperceptible.

—*Charles R. Swindoll*

The Downward Spiral
of Depravity

What you think determines what you do;
What you do determines what you become;
What you become determines what your life will be.

This cycle is a universal principle, and no book in the Bible illustrates this truth more dramatically than the book of Judges. Unfortunately, it's a negative illustration. We might call it *the downward spiral of depravity*.

The cycle always begins with a memory problem — forgetting about the Lord's mercy, grace, and blessings (Judges 3:7). Such shortsightedness leads to sinful attitudes and actions. When God's people no longer live according to God's standards, we live according to our own. Because we are sinful by nature, we tend to do evil and not good (3:7). When we persist in our sinfulness and refuse to repent, the Lord allows us to experience sin's consequences (3:8). Our sin becomes our master, chaining us in the dark pit of guilt. It usually takes the pit to persuade us to cry out in supplication (3:9). And because our God is a God of mercy and grace, He hears our pleas and empowers us to walk in righteousness through the Holy Spirit (3:9–10). Then, thankfully, a peaceful silence fills our souls (3:11) . . . until our memories grow short again.

But we don't have to repeat the cycle! Not if we remember the Lord's deliverance and live gratefully in light of that memory.

Week 16

Monday: Samson's Wandering, Weakness, and Collapse
- ☐ Judges 14–16
- ☐ Psalm 71

Tuesday: When God's People Descend to Decadence
- ☐ Judges 17–19
- ☐ Psalm 72

Wednesday: Bringing Justice to a Land without Absolutes
- ☐ Judges 20–21
- ☐ Psalm 73

Thursday: Redemptive Grace in a Difficult Time
- ☐ Ruth 1–4
- ☐ Psalm 74

Friday: Giving a Child Back to God, the Giver
- ☐ 1 Samuel 1–3
- ☐ Psalm 75

What I Want to Remember . . .

_____

_____

_____

_____

_____

Ignore righteousness long enough and depravity will breed the illegitimate child of permissiveness that says wrong is right.
— *Charles R. Swindoll*

Living with Absolutes in a World without Them

As night fell, the Levite's servant pointed eastward and asked if their small party should take refuge in the pagan city of Jebus (Judges 19:1–20). Refusing, the Levite suggested they press on further north: "We will not turn aside into the city of foreigners who are not of the sons of Israel" (19:12). The irony of his statement surfaced soon after, as the debauched night they spent in the Israelite city of Gibeah rivaled the decadence of Sodom and Gomorrah.

Tragically, in the place where righteousness should have shone, none existed.

Repeatedly, the book of Judges notes that Israel had no king in those days (18:1; 19:1; 21:25), which means the people had no one to enforce a moral standard. The book ends in the town of Gibeah from which came Saul, Israel's first king. As apples fall close to the tree, so Saul reflected his city's lack of absolutes in his reckless rule.

As God's people today, we also live in a land without absolutes—a culture in which the only standard not tolerated is intolerance. In such a context, the contrast Christians display comes from leading holy lives that reflect the holy God whom we worship (Matthew 5:16; Philippians 2:15; 1 Peter 2:12).

When we as Christians exhibit God's character, we provide a pathway to the refuge people expect from God's people . . . and the one they so desperately need.[4]

Week 17

Monday: God's Grace amid Staggering Defeat
- ☐ 1 Samuel 4–6
- ☐ Psalm 76

Tuesday: A Misguided Desire to Imitate the Nations
- ☐ 1 Samuel 7–9
- ☐ Psalm 77

Wednesday: The People's King Rises to Power
- ☐ 1 Samuel 10–12
- ☐ Psalm 78:1–16

Thursday: The People's King Falters
- ☐ 1 Samuel 13–15
- ☐ Psalm 78:17–33

Friday: God Looks at the Heart of His New Choice for King
- ☐ 1 Samuel 16–18
- ☐ Psalm 78:34–53

What I Want to Remember . . .

_____

_____

_____

_____

_____

Saul was tall. Saul was handsome. Saul was the people's choice to be the king, and God permitted them to select him. He began well. But slowly, silently, and subtly, Saul experienced the devastating effects of erosion.

—Charles R. Swindoll

A Spreading Fear

The destructive power of fear took center stage during a climactic period in Saul's failed reign. Saul triggered a cycle of fear when, afraid of the people, he disobeyed the prophet Samuel's clear command to put all the Amelekites to death (1 Samuel 15:24). Samuel's subsequent rebuke of Saul only added to the king's fear of his subjects.

As a result of Saul's failure, Samuel rightly parted ways with Saul for good. But when God prompted Samuel to go out and anoint another king, Samuel feared for his life, wondering whether or not Saul would try to kill him (16:2). Holed up alone at his home in Ramah, Samuel temporarily let his anxieties get the better of him.

Fear spread from the king of Israel to the prophet of Israel and ultimately to the people of Israel. Samuel eventually obeyed the Lord and traveled to Bethlehem. The elders of that town wondered anxiously whether or not the prophet had come in peace (16:4). No doubt, word had leaked out that Samuel had killed the Amelekite king (15:33), and the prophet's new bloody reputation preceded him.

Note the cycle of fear: the people inspired fear in Saul, Saul inspired fear in Samuel, and Samuel inspired fear in the people. If only one of these three had placed their confidence in the Lord, the cycle would have been broken.

Week 18

Monday: Friendship Defined: Jonathan and David
- ☐ 1 Samuel 19–21
- ☐ Psalm 78:54–72

Tuesday: David the Fugitive: On the Run from a Madman
- ☐ 1 Samuel 22–24
- ☐ Psalm 79

Wednesday: Abigail Saves Both Her Men
- ☐ 1 Samuel 25–27
- ☐ Psalm 80

Thursday: The Desperate End of a Desperate Man
- ☐ 1 Samuel 28–31
- ☐ Psalm 81

Friday: David Is Finally Anointed King of Judah
- ☐ 2 Samuel 1–3
- ☐ Psalm 82

What I Want to Remember . . .

_____

_____

_____

_____

When David was a fugitive in the wilderness, on the run from insanely jealous King Saul, he wrote some of his best stuff in the book of Psalms. It's been true in your life, too, hasn't it? In the hardest of times, you can often produce the best work, because you are most dependent on God.

—Charles R. Swindoll

Friendship

When the searing rays of adversity burn their way into our lives, a true friend brings relief like a sheltering tree.

David was hunted and haunted by madman Saul. The king's single objective was to see David dead. Between Saul and David, however, stood a sheltering tree named Jonathan.

Loyal and dependable, Jonathan assured David, "Whatever you say, I will do for you" (1 Samuel 20:4). No limits. No conditions. No bargains. No reservations. Best of all, when things were at their worst, Jonathan "went to David . . . and encouraged him in God" (23:16).

Why? Why would Jonathan, King Saul's son, risk his life to provide such refreshment? Because Jonathan was committed to the basic principles of a friendship. Because he "loved [David] as [he loved] himself" (18:1). It was love that knit their hearts together. The kind of love that causes people to lay down their lives for their friends, as Jesus put it (John 15:13). No greater love exists on this globe.

Beneath whose branches are *you* sheltered? Who rests beneath *yours*? Let's be busy about the business of watering and pruning and cultivating our friendships—even planting a few. Growing them takes time . . . but we will need them when the heat rises and the winds begin to blow.

Week 19

Monday: All Hail the King Who Dances before the Lord
- ☐ 2 Samuel 4–6
- ☐ Psalm 83

Tuesday: A Dream Deferred and a Dream Fulfilled
- ☐ 2 Samuel 7–9
- ☐ Psalm 84

Wednesday: Bathsheba's Bath and David's Decline
- ☐ 2 Samuel 10–12
- ☐ Psalm 85

Thursday: A Passive King and a Cunning Prince
- ☐ 2 Samuel 13–15
- ☐ Psalm 86

Friday: A Dead Dog's Bark and a Proud Prince's Death
- ☐ 2 Samuel 16–18
- ☐ Psalm 87

What I Want to Remember . . .

_____

_____

_____

_____

To David, not being allowed to build God's temple was the death of a dream. Perhaps your heart still stings when you remember a request to which God answered no. Follow David's model and say, "May Your name be magnified with or without a temple. May my life magnify You."
—Charles R. Swindoll

WHEN DREAMS DIE

King David's idea of building a temple for God struck the prophet Nathan like a thunderbolt. *God's gonna love this!* A magnificent temple to God would serve as a capstone for the capital city of Jerusalem.

So, Nathan gave David the go-ahead. But Nathan forgot to ask God. One evening, the Lord told Nathan that David wasn't the man to build a temple after all. David's son was.

David was heartbroken when he heard the news, but his response was heartwarming. David went before the Lord in prayer, focusing on God's complete control over his life and using the phrase "O Lord God" eight times. David also expressed his complete humility before God, calling himself "Your servant" ten times. Finally, David acknowledged that the dream of a temple was not for him alone but for God's glory (2 Samuel 7:18–29).

God's control . . . our humility . . . and God's glory. All dreamers should keep David's three-pronged prayer in mind as we submit our goals and our lives to the sovereignty of God and seek the glory of God with both.

Week 20

Monday: Rebellion, Revolt, Revenge . . . Restoration
- ☐ 2 Samuel 19–21
- ☐ Psalm 88

Tuesday: Praise, Pride, Pestilence . . . and a Place to Worship
- ☐ 2 Samuel 22–24
- ☐ Psalm 89:1–18

Wednesday: From War to Wisdom: David to Solomon
- ☐ 1 Kings 1–2
- ☐ Psalm 89:19–37

Thursday: Warnings to a Wise and Wealthy Individual
- ☐ 1 Kings 3–4
- ☐ Psalm 89:38–52

Friday: Building a Place for Worship
- ☐ 1 Kings 5–7
- ☐ Psalm 90

What I Want to Remember . . .

_____

_____

_____

_____

No heart is suddenly turned away. Solomon's heart slowly turned from honoring God to honoring his own desires. . . . If you're there right now, turn back! No one who has slipped needs to stay in that condition. The provision of grace says God can get you out.

—Charles R. Swindoll

Unwise Cracks

Solomon literally wrote the book on wisdom, and yet he behaved like a fool. How could anybody so wise let himself become so corrupted? It started with small compromises: "Solomon formed a marriage alliance with Pharaoh king of Egypt. . . . Solomon loved the LORD . . . *except* he sacrificed and burned incense on the high places" (1 Kings 3:1, 3, emphasis added).

Small compromises, sure. But they opened a crack in Solomon's heart that eventually divided it. The Canaanites sacrificed on hilltops because they felt "high places" brought them closer to their gods. The Israelites adopted this practice in sacrificing to the Lord, although God's Law forbade it. Also, Solomon's marriage to a nonbeliever attempted to buy national security for the price of a wedding.

He should have seen it coming. Solomon's poetry repeatedly revealed the wisdom of dealing with sin while it's still small (Proverbs 17:14; 24:33 – 34; Ecclesiastes 10:18; Song of Solomon 2:15). The crack that divided Solomon's heart would ultimately divide his nation, destroy God's temple, and deport the Hebrews from their land — and it all began with small sins ignored. Even wisdom can't prevent the consequences of compromise.

Solomon never started out to build pagan shrines. However, his failure to deal with the tiny cracks in his heart produced a life of futility and spiritual devastation. Solomon's life reveals that a sin tolerated becomes an idol embraced.

If we do not seek God as the object of our ultimate delight, we will certainly substitute the pursuits of this world — and eventually, even sacrifice our lives for them.[5]

Week 21

Monday: Dedicating a Place of Worship to God
- ☐ 1 Kings 8–9
- ☐ Psalm 91

Tuesday: Solomon Raised in Glory . . . and the Sin That Brought Him Low
- ☐ 1 Kings 10–12
- ☐ Psalm 92

Wednesday: A Kingdom Divided: On the Road to Destruction
- ☐ 1 Kings 13–15
- ☐ Psalm 93

Thursday: Doing Good in the Midst of an Evil People
- ☐ 1 Kings 16–18
- ☐ Psalm 94

Friday: Dealing with Discouragement
- ☐ 1 Kings 19–20
- ☐ Psalm 95

What I Want to Remember . . .

_____

_____

_____

_____

Isn't that just like the Lord? When life looked dreadful, when it looked as if the Israelites would never find a way out from under the sins of Ahab and Jezebel, along came Elijah.

—*Charles R. Swindoll*

He Did Evil in the Sight of the Lord

Let's admit it: sometimes reading through the books of 1 and 2 Kings can be a chore.

Whether it's a dull family tree, details about one unrecognizable king after another, or the latest in undermining an entire nation, these books recount some of the darkest and most difficult days in the history of Israel. Nothing embodies this difficulty more than the oft-repeated phrase, "He did evil in the sight of the Lord" (1 Kings 15:26).

For this section of Scripture, the old cliché applies: don't lose the forest for the trees. The gradual descent of Israel and Judah under their respective kings has to be placed in a larger biblical context. The historical books, especially those of 1 and 2 Kings, make clear the need for redemption. What goes down must come up.

Though God's people sinned repeatedly, He did not ultimately destroy or forget His people. Invasions? Yes. Exile? Absolutely. But in the end, He made sure that His people still had a real hope for the future.

This should give us confidence that whatever we as believers go through, God will not discard us. Life may be difficult. We may struggle in our fight against sin. But God is in the business of redeeming the sinful, of putting the broken back together again, and of making all things new.

Week 22

Monday: What Do You Do with a Wicked King?
- [ ] *1 Kings 21–22*
- [ ] *Psalm 96*

Tuesday: The End of an Era—in a Whirlwind!
- [ ] *2 Kings 1–3*
- [ ] *Psalm 97*

Wednesday: God Doesn't Forsake the Desperate
- [ ] *2 Kings 4–5*
- [ ] *Psalm 98*

Thursday: Treachery on the Throne, Turmoil in the Land
- [ ] *2 Kings 6–8*
- [ ] *Psalm 99*

Friday: Evil Never Wins in the End
- [ ] *2 Kings 9–10*
- [ ] *Psalm 100*

What I Want to Remember . . .

_____

_____

_____

_____

You need a place to be quiet and to listen to God's voice. It won't come in audible sounds. He has given us a Book. Take it along with you, open it, read it, close it up, and listen. You will hear things that I can't even describe. You will grow deep. You'll become more secure, more relieved of your anxiety. Do you have a place for that?

—Charles R. Swindoll

POTS OF OIL

When life takes a turn and your circumstances unfold in ways you hoped they never would, you know you need God.

In 2 Kings 4, we meet a single mom living on the edge of desperation. Her husband had suddenly died, leaving no inheritance. No income. And two young boys to feed. To make matters worse, they lived in a culture where children were made slaves if their parents couldn't pay the bills.

The fear factor was huge for this single mom. She needed help . . . and fast. She cried out to Elisha. Their exchange went something like this:

"What do you have left?" the prophet asked.

"Only a bit of oil."

"Gather as many pots as you can find. Ask your neighbors—ask for more than a few." And she did.

"Now, go inside, shut the door, and you and your boys pour your oil into these pots."

And they did.

And the oil flowed and flowed until every pot in the house was filled. When there were no more empty pots, the oil stopped.

In an economy where oil was as good as cash, the widow could now pay her debts.

You can be sure that when they returned their neighbors' pots, this single mom and her boys had a story to tell of God's deep compassion for desperate people facing desperate times. In faith they brought what they had to God, and He provided a miracle.

Week 23

Monday: A Boy King and an Assassination
- ☐ 2 Kings 11–14
- ☐ Psalm 101

Tuesday: Israel Cast Out of the Sight of the Lord
- ☐ 2 Kings 15–17
- ☐ Psalm 102

Wednesday: A King like No Other
- ☐ 2 Kings 18–19
- ☐ Psalm 103

Thursday: A Sick King, a Foolish Act, and the Word of God
- ☐ 2 Kings 20–22
- ☐ Psalm 104:1–17

Friday: O Jerusalem, Jerusalem—How the Mighty Has Fallen
- ☐ 2 Kings 23–25
- ☐ Psalm 104:18–35

What I Want to Remember . . .

_____

_____

_____

_____

_____

Sinning, despite warning, brings ruin without remedy. Inexcusable wrong brings inescapable wrath. Abused privilege incurs increased consequences.

—Charles R. Swindoll

The Missing Book

It had gone missing. Though no one realized it or knew how long it had been gone, when the Word of God was rediscovered, it moved the heart of a king.

Up until that point, King Josiah and the people of Judah had lived the truth of Amos 8:11:

> "I will send a famine on the land,
> Not a famine for bread or a thirst for water,
> But rather for hearing the words of the LORD."

Though they hadn't known of its absence, when they finally heard the words of this missing book, their response was like that of a man dying from thirst being given living water. They drank deeply from the well of the Word and humbled themselves in repentance and obedience (2 Kings 22:11–13; 23:1–3).

We live in a time and place where Bibles abound. Yet the Bible is missing — as if a spiritual famine has struck our land. Few of us can influence our culture as a king does his kingdom. Nevertheless, all of us, personally and within our families, can respond to God's Word as Josiah did.

We can humble ourselves under its counsel, repent of the sins it reveals, and obey its commandments.

Week 24

Monday: God's Faithfulness—from Adam to David
- ☐ *1 Chronicles 1–2*
- ☐ *Psalm 105:1–24*

Tuesday: David, Solomon, Jabez . . . and Significant Others
- ☐ *1 Chronicles 3–5*
- ☐ *Psalm 105:25–45*

Wednesday: Thank God for the Psalm Reading Today
- ☐ *1 Chronicles 6–7*
- ☐ *Psalm 106:1–15*

Thursday: Getting Ready for David as King
- ☐ *1 Chronicles 8–10*
- ☐ *Psalm 106:16–31*

Friday: Even the Godly Must Follow God's Word
- ☐ *1 Chronicles 11–13*
- ☐ *Psalm 106:32–48*

What I Want to Remember . . .

_____

_____

_____

_____

God never intended to make a best seller out of 1 and 2 Chronicles. But they are absolutely essential for the Book of God to be complete. They are for our faith what the telephone book is for our communication. These are reference books of God's dealing with people throughout history.
—Charles R. Swindoll

From Trouble to Triumph

Some places evoke bad memories. The Valley of Achor was such a site. After Joshua's victory at Jericho, the Israelites suffered defeat at Ai because a man named Achan had buried banned spoils of war under his tent (Joshua 7:1, 21).

The word *Achor* means "trouble," and so, with a slight variation of Achan's name, Joshua asked him, "Why have you *troubled* us?" (7:25, emphasis added). After Achan's execution, the valley where he died took on the name "Valley of Achor."

When the original readers of 1 Chronicles came across this story in the genealogical record, they would have remembered Achan as Achar, "the troubler" (1 Chronicles 2:7). But they also would have recalled that the prophets described the Valley of Achor—a place once linked with sin, discipline, and death—as a place of promise. Hosea spoke of the valley as a future "door of hope" and a place for joyful singing (Hosea 2:15). Isaiah referred to the dry valley as the spot where herds will someday rest (Isaiah 65:10).

God can produce hope in spite of our awful situations. We allow Him to do this by coming to terms with our willful sin. We have the promise that when we confess our buried, hidden sins, God will purify us from all unrighteousness—even from those sins buried so deep we don't know to confess them (1 John 1:9).

God can change our "trouble" into triumph, but first we must come clean.[6]

Week 25

Monday: Creating Space for the Ark: The Centrality of Worship
- [ ] 1 Chronicles 14–16
- [ ] Psalm 107:1–16

Tuesday: A Promise from God and a Kingdom Solidified
- [ ] 1 Chronicles 17–19
- [ ] Psalm 107:17–32

Wednesday: Worship: The Response to Sin and Suffering
- [ ] 1 Chronicles 20–22
- [ ] Psalm 107:33–43

Thursday: Solomon Divides the Responsibilities for Worship
- [ ] 1 Chronicles 23–25
- [ ] Psalm 108

Friday: Solomon Divides Government and Military Responsibilities
- [ ] 1 Chronicles 26–27
- [ ] Psalm 109

What I Want to Remember . . .

_____

_____

_____

_____

In 1 Chronicles, two forces are continually at work: the compassion of God and the rebellion of man. God keeps being faithful and compassionate; the people keep mocking and despising.

—*Charles R. Swindoll*

"LET HIS PRAYER BECOME SIN": DAVID'S THIRST FOR VENGEANCE

Burning anger. Intense hurt. A longing for vengeance.

No doubt you've grappled with these feelings at some point in your life. And you're not alone. They are typical reactions of victims of wrongdoing.

Even a man after God's own heart, King David, recorded intense responses like these in the Psalms. In Psalm 109, David's rage is hard to ignore. He asked God to take his enemy's life, to make the man's children beggars, and even that this man's prayer would "become sin" (Psalm 109:6–10).

Living in this age where God mercifully delays His return so that more people might be saved, how is a Christian to interpret and apply such biting pronouncements? First, the Bible makes clear that vengeance belongs to the Lord (Deuteronomy 32:35; Psalm 94:1). That David *prayed* his thoughts of vengeance shows that he affirmed God's responsibility in his situation.

Second, as Christians, we believe that God poured out on Jesus His vengeance and judgment for the sin of humanity. Our belief in the saving power of Jesus's crucifixion is, in part, a profound recognition of our own sin against God. In this light, psalms such as 109 become more about the struggle with ourselves than they are about our enemies.

These psalms remind us in vivid detail of both the judgment we deserve and the compassion God provides.

Week 26

Monday: Temple Plans and Dreams
- ☐ 1 Chronicles 28–29
- ☐ Psalm 110

Tuesday: What a King Who Has Everything Needs
- ☐ 2 Chronicles 1–3
- ☐ Psalm 111

Wednesday: Building the Place Where God Dwells
- ☐ 2 Chronicles 4–5
- ☐ Psalm 112

Thursday: Solomon's Magnificent Prayer
- ☐ 2 Chronicles 6–8
- ☐ Psalm 113

Friday: A Royal Visit from the Queen Next Door
- ☐ 2 Chronicles 9–11
- ☐ Psalm 114

What I Want to Remember . . .

_____

_____

_____

_____

_____

The underlying message of Chronicles: Remember! Oh, it's so easy to forget. It's so easy to faint. May you see God's hand in the land of the living and learn the lesson that others have forgotten along the way.
—Charles R. Swindoll

THE GLORY OF THE LORD

Before his addiction to the glamour of the kingdom, the allure of women and wine, and the power plays of politics, Solomon's heart beat after God. Like his dad before him and like no son after him, Solomon walked with God . . . for a time.

The pinnacle of Solomon's life achievements and the desire of his heart in those early years was the completion of the temple. Read of his passion and delight in pleasing the Lord in his temple dedication prayer in 2 Chronicles 6, one of the longest and deepest prayers in the Bible. God's response to Solomon's devotion was dramatic and never again duplicated. When the temple construction was complete, "fire came down from heaven and consumed the . . . sacrifices, and the glory of the LORD filled the temple" (2 Chronicles 7:1 NIV). The atmosphere was so awesome that no one could even enter the temple. People fell to the ground in worship and thanks, repeating, "He is good; his love endures forever" (7:3 NIV). It was a moment for the ages.

No doubt Solomon pondered that memory years later when his heart for God had cooled with selfishness and overindulgence. As he poured himself another drink, he most likely remembered—or tried to forget—what it was like to be consumed with passion for the things of God. In his lonely palace where he had once led God's people with wisdom, you might have heard his whispers of regret, "Above all else, guard your heart" (Proverbs 4:23 NIV).

Week 27

Monday: Judah and Israel's Civil War
- ☐ 2 Chronicles 12–13
- ☐ Psalm 115

Tuesday: Asa Learns to Trust the Hard Way
- ☐ 2 Chronicles 14–16
- ☐ Psalm 116

Wednesday: Jehoshaphat—What a Great Leader!
- ☐ 2 Chronicles 17–19
- ☐ Psalm 117

Thursday: Jehoshaphat's Success . . . Jehoram and Ahaziah's Failure
- ☐ 2 Chronicles 20–22
- ☐ Psalm 118

Friday: Joash and Amaziah, Godly Kings . . . *Sort Of*
- ☐ 2 Chronicles 23–25
- ☐ Psalm 119:1–16

What I Want to Remember . . .

_____

_____

_____

_____

Is your heart fully committed to God? Choose one area of reservation and invite the Spirit of God to break through and to create something new in your life. Turn your prayers in the direction of surrender, rather than defense. God will strengthen you in that attitude.

—Charles R. Swindoll

LEARNING TO TRUST GOD ALONE

King Asa trusted the Lord in a battle against an army a million strong (2 Chronicles 14:9–15). But when King Baasha built up the city of Ramah—which sat only five miles north of Jerusalem—he effectively blockaded all movement into Asa's land. Regrettably, Asa's faith weakened, and he took riches from the treasuries of the temple to solicit help from the pagan king of Aram (16:1–6).

Why would Asa, who earlier had the faith to defeat a million men, panic and look to his own devices? Because God took from Asa something precious—a parcel of land. Asa felt vulnerable without the strategic plateau surrounding Ramah. So he scrambled to regain it at all costs.

We often have no problem trusting God in those areas of life where we *already* trust Him. We can seem so spiritual in our comfort zones! But what do we do when God requires of us our most precious possessions or people?

We learn from Asa that God may remove what we depend on so that we will learn to trust God alone. As Hanani said to Asa, "The eyes of the Lord move to and fro throughout the earth that He may strongly support those whose heart is completely His" (16:9).

God wants our trust, in part, so that He may do marvelous deeds in our lives.[7]

Week 28

Monday: How God Deals with Arrogance
- ☐ 2 Chronicles 26–28
- ☐ Psalm 119:17–32

Tuesday: How God Deals with Faithfulness
- ☐ 2 Chronicles 29–31
- ☐ Psalm 119:33–48

Wednesday: Like Father, Not Like Son
- ☐ 2 Chronicles 32–33
- ☐ Psalm 119:49–64

Thursday: The End of an Era
- ☐ 2 Chronicles 34–36
- ☐ Psalm 119:65–80

Friday: Returning, Rebuilding, Restoring
- ☐ Ezra 1–3
- ☐ Psalm 119:81–96

What I Want to Remember . . .

_____

_____

_____

_____

_____

_____

What influenced Josiah to be such a contrast to his times? It was the Word of God, which Josiah found and followed. Josiah embraced Scripture without reservation as he cultivated a heart for God.

—Charles R. Swindoll

Breaking the Generational Curse

It's tough coming from a family that doesn't honor God.

Josiah's father and grandfather were two of Judah's worst kings. When Josiah heard the Scriptures for the first time, he reacted in immediate sorrow: "Our fathers have not observed the word of the LORD, to do according to all that is written in this book" (2 Chronicles 34:21).

So Josiah determined to be different.

Josiah removed from God's dilapidated temple everything that was pagan, burning it all in the valley outside Jerusalem. Not only did Josiah remove what was wrong, he also began doing what was right. He initiated repair on the temple of God. He gave instructions for the people to observe the Passover in strict accordance with Scripture. In fact, that year they celebrated a Passover the likes of which had not been seen for hundreds of years!

In short, Josiah tore down all that competed with the worship of God, and he built up that which assisted it.

We can learn from Josiah that our model for life must be God's Word, not our parents' examples. Living in the backwash of our parents' sins does not allow us the excuse or justification to repeat those mistakes. We must acknowledge our pain, grieve the losses, and call sin what it is. But then we can't let righteous anger fester into unrighteous actions. It has to stop somewhere.

Like Josiah, we must determine to walk faithfully in our *own* generation by tearing down all that competes with our worship of God and by building up that which assists it.

Week 29

Monday: Overcoming Hindrances to Worship
- [ ] Ezra 4–6
- [ ] Psalm 119:97–112

Tuesday: A Remnant Confesses Their Sin before the Lord
- [ ] Ezra 7–10
- [ ] Psalm 119:113–128

Wednesday: Rebuilding the Holy City
- [ ] Nehemiah 1–3
- [ ] Psalm 119:129–144

Thursday: Dealing with Opposition to God's Work
- [ ] Nehemiah 4–6
- [ ] Psalm 119:145–160

Friday: Celebrating the Completion of Good Work
- [ ] Nehemiah 7–9
- [ ] Psalm 119:161–176

What I Want to Remember . . .

_____

_____

_____

_____

Nehemiah was a man who faced reality but never lost his motivation. He dealt with constant disappointment, attack, persecution, affliction, and being knocked down. But he refused to be knocked out. What a magnificent model of determination!

—*Charles R. Swindoll*

Building Resistance

From the moment Nehemiah arrived in Jerusalem, he experienced resistance.

He had served in Babylon as the king's cupbearer, but after petitioning first the Lord and then the king on behalf of the struggling Jews in Jerusalem, Nehemiah traveled to the holy city (Nehemiah 1:11–2:5).

The former royal servant organized teams to rebuild the walls that stretched around Jerusalem, walls which had lain broken and burned since the Babylonian invasion some seventy years prior. However, a group of locals from surrounding cities, led by Sanballat and Tobiah, opposed the building project. First, they mocked the builders, and when that didn't work, they threatened violent conflict (4:1–8).

In the face of resistance, Nehemiah and his people stood strong. They expressed their dependence on God by praying (4:9). But after that? They acted.

Nehemiah stationed guards, and the workers took up weapons. And they continued to build. With each stone laid and each gap closed, minute after minute and day after day, the Jewish people added weight and strength to their resistance. As the wall grew, so did their courage. The Jews would not allow the mockers on the sidelines to control their destiny.

God's people persevered in their work. The result? They completed the wall and looked forward to a renewal of life in the city of God.

Week 30

Monday: Who's Who List in the Rebuilt Jerusalem
- [ ] *Nehemiah 10–11*
- [ ] *Psalm 120*

Tuesday: Final Details in the Rebuilding Project
- [ ] *Nehemiah 12–13*
- [ ] *Psalm 121*

Wednesday: Fairy Tale Gone Wrong
- [ ] *Esther 1–3*
- [ ] *Psalm 122*

Thursday: To Be Used . . . Whatever the Cost
- [ ] *Esther 4–7*
- [ ] *Psalm 123*

Friday: A Happy Ending
- [ ] *Esther 8–10*
- [ ] *Psalm 124*

What I Want to Remember . . .

_____

_____

_____

_____

_____

The workings of God are related to your crises but unrelated to your clock. So while waiting, look beyond the present. Do you know the best way to do that? Pray!

—*Charles R. Swindoll*

Courage under Fire

No one is born courageous.

Esther learned about courage from her uncle, Mordecai. He boldly stuck to his convictions by refusing to bow to the wicked Haman. Later, Mordecai challenged Esther to do what she could to save their people when Haman conspired to murder every Jew in Persia, a problem old and familiar to the Jews.

Esther knew it would take more than courage to fix this problem. She threw herself on God's mercy. She asked her uncle to get all the Jews in the land to fast for her. "My maidens and I will do the same," she said.

As much as they needed food, they needed God's help more. So they fasted. And they waited. And they prayed.

As she stormed God's presence during those three days, the Lord gripped Esther's heart and she became unafraid of what she faced. She allowed Him to guide her thoughts and help frame her words and actions at a time when her life — and subsequently the lives of thousands of God's people — was at risk. This period of pleading with God was a silent yet powerful parenthesis in her life.

In God's apparent absence, God's people discovered Him at work, moving in a thousand places at the same time, working in circumstances beyond their control and outside their observation — protecting, providing, and orchestrating people and events for His great purposes.

Such is His work today.

Week 31

Monday: God Trusts Job, but Job Questions God's Judgment
- ☐ *Job 1–3*
- ☐ *Psalm 125*

Tuesday: "The Problem Lies in Job's Sin," but Job Still Questions
- ☐ *Job 4–7*
- ☐ *Psalm 126*

Wednesday: "The Problem Lies in Job's Faith," but Job Still Questions
- ☐ *Job 8–10*
- ☐ *Psalm 127*

Thursday: "The Problem Lies in Job's Pride," but Job Questions His Friends
- ☐ *Job 11–14*
- ☐ *Psalm 128*

Friday: "It Must Be Job's Fault," but Job Demands God's Testimony
- ☐ *Job 15–17*
- ☐ *Psalm 129*

What I Want to Remember . . .

_____

_____

_____

———— ✦ ————

What comes from the Lord because it is impossible for humans to manufacture it? Wisdom. What comes from humans because it is impossible for the Lord to experience it? Worry. What is it that brings wisdom and dispels worry? Worship.

—Charles R. Swindoll

LIFE IN THE WHIRLWIND

The irony of Job's situation was lost on him. He lived through the whirlwind of his trials without the privilege of reading the first three chapters of the book that bears his name. He trusted God, but he had no idea that God trusted him enough to offer him as a test case of faithfulness (Job 1:1, 8). As far as Job could see, his life was at best an oversight on God's part and at worst a tragic injustice (3:11–16; 20–26).

The expression "the patience of Job" fails to describe the way Job felt about his situation or the way in which he handled it! He was constantly questioning and often *impatient*. He was driven to make his case — to be heard in the supreme court of heaven.

Job's friends didn't help matters much. They had knowledge enough to know that God judges sinners. Therefore — in their reasoning — Job must have been out of favor with God to deserve such misery. But Job had wisdom enough to know that his misery was not warranted in those terms. "It's not fair!" was his cry.

God's sovereignty extends beyond our seeing and our knowing. His ways are always just and always good for those who trust Him, even if we cannot see the wisdom behind His plan.

Week 32

Monday: Reassurance and Hope for the Hurting
- ☐ *Job 18–19*
- ☐ *Psalm 130*

Tuesday: Responding with Wisdom to Unfair Accusations
- ☐ *Job 20–21*
- ☐ *Psalm 131*

Wednesday: Handling Criticism with Grace
- ☐ *Job 22–24*
- ☐ *Psalm 132*

Thursday: Straining to Understand God
- ☐ *Job 25–27*
- ☐ *Psalm 133*

Friday: Words from an Innocent Man
- ☐ *Job 28–31*
- ☐ *Psalm 134*

What I Want to Remember . . .

_____

_____

_____

David compared the spiritual blessing of a united people centered in Zion—the place of worship—with the physical blessing of dew from Mount Hermon. The bond that believers have in Christ can bring about this same kind of blessing. In spite of differences in style, language, culture, color, and education, Christians from all around the world can live together in harmony.

—Charles R. Swindoll

THE BLESSING OF UNITY

King David experienced revolts, rebellions, and numerous family squabbles. He knew what he was talking about when he wrote in Psalm 133:1:

> How good and how pleasant it is
> For brothers to dwell together in unity!

David compared the blessing of unity to precious oil that anoints the head of the high priest. So much oil, in fact, that it drips off the priest's robes! That's a lot of blessing.

David also linked unity to the melting snows of Mount Hermon, which form the headwaters of the Jordan River. In describing "the dew of Hermon" (Psalm 133:3), David referred to that area's abundant streams reaching the dry mountains of Zion, something that never occurs geographically. But the hyperbole suggests, "Imagine if it *did* happen!" The blessing of harmony is like a multitude of cool, refreshing streams that flow in places that desperately need it.

Unity is "good and pleasant" but, sadly, also infrequent. Though David's aggravated son Absalom returned to live in Jerusalem for two years, the two men never spoke a word (2 Samuel 14:28). There's a big difference between dwelling together and dwelling together *in unity*.

Many a home houses those who dwell together. Most churches contain believers who worship under the same roof. But failing to dwell together in peace is like wasting gallons of olive oil or streams of fresh water. What's more, by failing to get along with others, we obstruct our own relationship with God (1 Peter 3:7; 1 John 4:20).

Unity begins with personal humility and genuine forgiveness. And the results? Overflowing *blessing* . . . directly from God.[8]

Week 33

Monday: Youthful Indignation on Display
- ☐ Job 32–34
- ☐ Psalm 135

Tuesday: Defending God's Honor
- ☐ Job 35–37
- ☐ Psalm 136

Wednesday: God Questions Job from the Storm
- ☐ Job 38–39
- ☐ Psalm 137

Thursday: Repentance in the Face of God's Greatness
- ☐ Job 40–42
- ☐ Psalm 138

Friday: The Meaningless Pursuits of This Life
- ☐ Ecclesiastes 1–3
- ☐ Psalm 139

What I Want to Remember . . .

_____

_____

_____

_____

_____

We never forget God's whirlwind messages. Most of us could testify that our lives began to be changed because of a reproof that came through some enormously significant event, usually a stormy one.

—Charles R. Swindoll

God's Mysterious Answer to Suffering

He lost all his assets. His servants perished at the hands of bandits. His children fell victim to natural disaster. He even suffered the physical pain of disease. Job, despite being blameless and upright in the sight of God, lost virtually everything in a single day.

Even with grief weighing on him heavier than all the sands of the seas, Job worshiped God (Job 1:20, 6:2–3). But he also expressed his desire for God to kill him (6:8–9) and openly longed to present his case before the Lord face-to-face, like a man before a judge (23:3–7).

Job received that wish. However, their encounter occurred in a way wholly unexpected. God appeared in the midst of a whirlwind. And rather than listen to Job present his case, God Himself chose to speak—not with answers to Job's questions but with questions of His own.

Beginning in Job 38, God asked Job seventy-seven different questions. In the aftermath of this newest storm in Job's life, the suffering man was left only to admit his lack of understanding and to repent of his presumptuousness (42:1–6).

The lesson is clear: though suffering is clearly an intrusion in God's good world, the Lord uses suffering to humble us that we might strengthen our trust in Him and steel our obedience to His commands.

Week 34

Monday: Satisfaction at the Mall?
- ☐ *Ecclesiastes 4–6*
- ☐ *Psalm 140*

Tuesday: The Beauty of Wisdom
- ☐ *Ecclesiastes 7–9*
- ☐ *Psalm 141*

Wednesday: The Conclusion of the Matter
- ☐ *Ecclesiastes 10–12*
- ☐ *Psalm 142*

Thursday: I Am My Beloved's
- ☐ *Song of Solomon 1–4*
- ☐ *Psalm 143*

Friday: The Joys of Married Life
- ☐ *Song of Solomon 5–8*
- ☐ *Psalm 144*

What I Want to Remember . . .

_____

_____

_____

_____

_____

The lure of something better is always with us. Listen to the commercials, read the media, and you will hear the pulsating push for something more. Solomon says, "Without God, nothing will satisfy. Nothing!"

—Charles R. Swindoll

Under the Sun

There once lived a man who had the time, money, and energy to explore every facet of life in search of meaning and purpose. Solomon was free to walk wherever he wanted. No one restrained him, and he held nothing back. Thankfully, he kept an accurate journal of his journey, which is available for all to read in the book named Ecclesiastes.

But the journey Solomon took, while mind-boggling at first, eventually left him depressed and disillusioned. His favorite word: *empty*. Nothing satisfied. Nothing he saw, discovered, attempted, or concluded as a result of his lengthy search resulted in lasting significance or personal satisfaction. He came up . . . empty.

But wait. Why was life such a pointless treadmill for Solomon? Why couldn't the man who was king, who had such an endless supply of financial resources, find something—*anything*—that had purpose?

To quote from Solomon's own testimony, it was because of his "under-the-sun" perspective. Time after time, Solomon mentioned his horizontal, strictly human viewpoint. Because he seldom looked above the sun to find reassurance, life seemed hopelessly meaningless. He went to great lengths to find happiness, but because he left God out of the picture, nothing satisfied.

It never will. Satisfaction under the sun will never happen until we have a meaningful connection with the living Lord above the sun.

Week 35

Monday: Enough Is Enough, People!
- ☐ *Isaiah 1–2*
- ☐ *Psalm 145*

Tuesday: Out with the Old and In with the New
- ☐ *Isaiah 3–5*
- ☐ *Psalm 146*

Wednesday: Isaiah's Call . . . Immanuel's Coming
- ☐ *Isaiah 6–8*
- ☐ *Psalm 147*

Thursday: God's Magnificent Promise of Messiah
- ☐ *Isaiah 9–11*
- ☐ *Psalm 148*

Friday: Israel's Hope Looks Good—Israel's Enemies? Not Good.
- ☐ *Isaiah 12–14*
- ☐ *Psalm 149*

What I Want to Remember . . .

_____

_____

_____

_____

If we, like Isaiah, saw the Lord while still earthbound, we would instantly realize our lack of holiness. We would see Him in His impeccable purity and we would immediately be made aware of those soiled splotches of our lives that needing cleansing.

—*Charles R. Swindoll*

Benjamin in Between

The sibling rivalry among the sons of Jacob passed through succeeding generations like an inherited disease.

These twelve sons produced twelve tribes, and two of these tribes dominated the contention. Judah—the tribe from which the Messiah would come—and Ephraim—a tribe from Jacob's favorite son, Joseph—continually locked horns over national control.

Consequently, when Israel settled in Canaan, God positioned a buffer between Judah and Ephraim—the little tribe of Benjamin (Joshua 18:5, 11). The "buffer zone" of Benjamin possessed an enviable plateau with strategic crossroads that remained the constant desire of these dominant tribes. Israel's first king, Saul, hailed from Benjamin. King David relocated from the territory of Judah to Benjamin, choosing neutral Jerusalem as his capital. These events served to unify the nation by keeping peace between the north and the south. But even in a united Israel, the rivalry never ceased.

The prophet Isaiah looked ahead to when Judah and Ephraim would together defeat God's enemies via routes over the land of Benjamin (Isaiah 11:13–14). Finally, they would serve a cause higher than themselves—that of the kingdom of God.

Like Benjamin in between, we are called by God to be peacemakers (Matthew 5:9; Romans 12:18; James 3:14–4:1). As believers anticipating God's kingdom, we serve a purpose higher than our own agendas. Rather than envy what God has given another, we should remember the One who laid down His life for others—and then follow His example.[9]

Week 36

Monday: Bad News for Moab . . . Praise for the Lord
- ☐ *Isaiah 15–17*
- ☐ *Psalm 150*

Tuesday: Egypt, Ethiopia, and the Everlasting God
- ☐ *Isaiah 18–20*
- ☐ *Proverbs 1:1–7*

Wednesday: A Violent End Worth Noting
- ☐ *Isaiah 21–23*
- ☐ *Proverbs 1:8–19*

Thursday: Looking Forward to the Lord's Intervention
- ☐ *Isaiah 24–26*
- ☐ *Proverbs 1:20–33*

Friday: Special Words for the People of God
- ☐ *Isaiah 27–29*
- ☐ *Proverbs 2:1–9*

What I Want to Remember . . .

_____

_____

_____

_____

God wants our total trust. Nothing less. No games, no empty, pious-sounding words. He commands our absolute confidence. There is no area that He is unable to handle. God is a specialist in every circumstance— including yours.

—Charles R. Swindoll

A Highway for Worship

For thousands of years, an international highway stretched the full length of the land of Israel. All traffic, trade, or war with Egypt had to cross the soil of this Promised Land. Consequently, every reigning superpower also fought with Israel over control of this road.

In Isaiah's time, the superpower was Assyria. Israel considered turning to Egypt for help from the threat of Assyria. So Isaiah used the highway as an illustration of another day far in the future: "In that day there will be a highway from Egypt to Assyria" (Isaiah 19:23). The travelers on this road, however, would not have war on their minds—but worship.

In the future kingdom of God when Jesus Christ rules the earth from Israel, all nations will gather to worship Him. Isaiah shows that Egypt—the very nation which Judah wanted to run to for help—will one day turn to Judah instead and worship the Lord. Egypt will learn the Hebrew language, set up monuments to the Lord, and receive His blessing (19:18–19, 25).

Looking today at the Arab nations of Egypt and Iraq, this prophecy seems an absolute marvel, just as it must have seemed to the Hebrews in Isaiah's time. Yet Isaiah foretold that one day "every knee will bow, every tongue will swear allegiance" to the Lord (45:23), whom we know to be Jesus Christ (Philippians 2:10).

Imagine all nations traveling a highway to Israel to worship the Lord together! Then consider what a privilege we have to know the truth and to worship the Lord today.[10]

Week 37

Monday: Warnings against Alliances with Enemies
- ☐ *Isaiah 30–32*
- ☐ *Proverbs 2:10–22*

Tuesday: God Judges the Wicked, Bringing Relief to His Creation
- ☐ *Isaiah 33–35*
- ☐ *Proverbs 3:1–12*

Wednesday: Trusting in the Power of God, Not the Promise of Men.
- ☐ *Isaiah 36–39*
- ☐ *Proverbs 3:13–26*

Thursday: God's Greatness Brings Hope to Humanity
- ☐ *Isaiah 40–42*
- ☐ *Proverbs 3:27–35*

Friday: Redemption and Blessing Await God's People
- ☐ *Isaiah 43–44*
- ☐ *Proverbs 4:1–9*

What I Want to Remember . . .

_____

_____

_____

God doesn't dispense strength and encouragement like a pharmacist fills your prescription. The Lord doesn't promise to give us something to take so we can handle our weary moments. He promises us Himself. That is all. That is enough.

—Charles R. Swindoll

Redeeming the Land

In a famous biblical passage, the apostle Paul declared that though all creation has been "subjected to futility," it also looks forward to being "set free from its slavery to corruption" (Romans 8:20–21). In other words, creation itself bears the effects of human sin, and one day, when God's redemptive work has been completed, creation, too, will partake of God's glory.

Paul wasn't the only biblical writer to understand this. Some seven hundred years prior, the prophet Isaiah looked forward to the glorious day of redemption, using vivid imagery to portray the renewing of the physical world. Once the wicked have been removed from the earth and the land has been deeded to God's people,

> The wilderness and the desert will be glad . . .
> Like the crocus
> [The Arabah desert] will blossom profusely.
> (Isaiah 35:1–2)

We often think of redemption in strictly spiritual terms, as something that happens only to our souls. However, the Bible makes it clear that God will redeem the physical elements of creation as well. Isaiah 35 looks forward specifically to the Millennium, though our dwelling in the new heaven and the new earth will also be a decidedly physical one.

Both the seen and the unseen serve as factors in God's plan for the future. Let's make sure that both remain vital to us in the present as well.

Week 38

Monday: Don't Argue with God
- [ ] Isaiah 45–47
- [ ] Proverbs 4:10–19

Tuesday: The Promise of Restoration
- [ ] Isaiah 48–50
- [ ] Proverbs 4:20–27

Wednesday: The Suffering Servant Foretold
- [ ] Isaiah 51–53
- [ ] Proverbs 5:1–14

Thursday: Words of Hope for a Better Day
- [ ] Isaiah 54–56
- [ ] Proverbs 5:15–23

Friday: Rebuilding, Restoring, Redeeming
- [ ] Isaiah 57–59
- [ ] Proverbs 6:1–11

What I Want to Remember . . .

_____

_____

_____

_____

One of the marks of spiritual maturity is the quiet confidence that God is in control . . . without the need to understand why He does what He does. When you hope in the Lord—seeking Him, waiting on Him—you experience inner strength you never knew before.

—Charles R. Swindoll

God Is in Control

Isaiah knew what it was like to move among the arrogant, self-sufficient, and affluent people of his day. They had power, money, and influence—what more did they need? Life was moving along at a pretty comfortable pace—why did they need God?

Isaiah's message to them was, in effect, "Like it or not, you're not in control. God is the One who calls the shots. He is sovereign."

Sovereignty—what does that mean? God is invincible (He will always win), immutable (He won't ever change), omnipotent (He has the power to do anything), and self-sufficient (He needs nothing). God sees the end as clearly as the beginning. He has no rival on earth or in heaven. He entertains no fears, possesses no ignorance, has no needs, experiences no frustrations or limitations. God always knows what is best, always pursues the goal that is consistent with the best, and never makes a mistake in the process. Because God is sovereign, His judgments are unsearchable, His ways are unfathomable, and His will is unchangeable.

Because God is sovereign, He controls rather than suggests. He guides rather than guesses. He fulfills rather than dreams. He brings a perfect conclusion rather than merely hoping for the best.

That's why we need God. We can trust Him, even when He doesn't explain why. He doesn't have to . . . because He is sovereign.

Week 39

Monday: Good News for God's People
- [ ] Isaiah 60–63
- [ ] Proverbs 6:12–19

Tuesday: Mercy Given to Rebellious Hearts
- [ ] Isaiah 64–66
- [ ] Proverbs 6:20–35

Wednesday: Sniffing the Wind of Immorality
- [ ] Jeremiah 1–2
- [ ] Proverbs 7:1–5

Thursday: Lessons from the Harlot
- [ ] Jeremiah 3–4
- [ ] Proverbs 7:6–23

Friday: Destruction—the Results of Unfaithfulness
- [ ] Jeremiah 5–7
- [ ] Proverbs 7:24–27

What I Want to Remember . . .

_____

_____

_____

_____

Ignore God's Word, and the result is predictable: consequences of the most severe nature will fall upon you. I don't care how intelligent you are . . . how clever . . . how old . . . or how rich. Ignore God's Word, and you will pay a price—horrible consequences.

—Charles R. Swindoll

Go to Shiloh ... and See

Biblical history often repeats itself. The people of Judah in Jeremiah's day felt that because the temple in Jerusalem remained untouched for centuries, they also stood secure—in spite of their sin.

But the Lord told them otherwise: "Go now to My place which was in Shiloh . . . and see what I did to it" (Jeremiah 7:12). In going to ancient Shiloh, the people could see with their own eyes what happens when God's people trust in anything but Him.

Shiloh had once housed the tabernacle of Moses which stood strong for three hundred years. But the Lord allowed the Philistines to destroy the tabernacle because the Hebrews refused to trust in God (1 Samuel 4:10–11). The site seen by the people in Jeremiah's time was nothing but a pile of rubble.

The example proved prophetic. A mere twenty years after Jeremiah's words, the Babylonians demolished the temple in which Jeremiah's people had trusted . . . just like what had happened at Shiloh.

No doubt, we all place a premium on security. Retirement accounts, insurance policies, and alarm systems demand a significant chunk of our earnings. Prudent? Absolutely. But do these safeguards provide true protection? If God withdrew His hand, all of our protection, precautions, and safety measures would collapse in an instant (Job 1–2; Psalm 127:1).

Let's learn from Shiloh what Judah failed to understand. Let's place our trust in the Lord above all other securities.[11]

Week 40

Monday: The Thrill of Wisdom . . . the Agony of Deceit
- ☐ Jeremiah 8–10
- ☐ Proverbs 8:1–11

Tuesday: Jeremiah Takes On Jerusalem
- ☐ Jeremiah 11–13
- ☐ Proverbs 8:12–21

Wednesday: Praying and Wasted Prayers
- ☐ Jeremiah 14–16
- ☐ Proverbs 8:22–36

Thursday: Our Deceitful Hearts and Our Sovereign God
- ☐ Jeremiah 17–19
- ☐ Proverbs 9:1–12

Friday: Jeremiah's Capture, Complaint, and Caution
- ☐ Jeremiah 20–22
- ☐ Proverbs 9:13–18

What I Want to Remember . . .

_____

_____

_____

_____

_____

The secret of counteracting our bent toward waywardness rests with wisdom. . . . Wisdom is calling for our attention. She doesn't want us to drift throughout the day without taking her along as our close companion.
—Charles R. Swindoll

WISDOM IN OUR WAY

In stark contrast to the warnings in Proverbs 5–7 about how a man's lust for a woman produces death, Proverbs 8–9 points the naive to that which all other desirables can't compare: *wisdom*.

Solomon personifies wisdom as a woman calling out to men—a voice that leads them to life, not death. She positions herself at strategic locations they will certainly pass by. She chooses as her podium places where men cannot miss her message (Proverbs 8:1–3).

Wisdom still calls to us, men and women alike. She still stands in these prominent places, at crossroads of vulnerability in all of our lives. Walking near, we hear what we need before moving on. If we have the courage to listen—to *really* listen—wisdom can alter both our route and our resolution. Perhaps we stop. Or turn around. Maybe we continue on the right path . . . being challenged to keep at it.

But wisdom is not the only voice positioned at these strategic settings. The "woman of folly" also hollers her way into our attention and—if we're not careful—into our affections. Her siren's song of compromise has our ruin as its hidden ambition (9:13–18).

So God has put wisdom in our way—an unavoidable voice requiring all who pass by to make a choice. We have to step over wisdom, walk around her, or embrace her. But we cannot ignore that she is present.

God's wisdom, distilled in the pages of Scripture, invites us to yearn for her above any other lust or longing.[12]

Week 41

Monday: Hope for the Righteous . . . Captivity for the Wicked
- ☐ Jeremiah 23–25
- ☐ Proverbs 10:1–10

Tuesday: Serving a Wicked Master
- ☐ Jeremiah 26–27
- ☐ Proverbs 10:11–21

Wednesday: Speaking the Truth to Those in Exile
- ☐ Jeremiah 28–29
- ☐ Proverbs 10:22–32

Thursday: Mourning Turned to Joy
- ☐ Jeremiah 30–31
- ☐ Proverbs 11:1–11

Friday: Restoration Will Follow Captivity
- ☐ Jeremiah 32–33
- ☐ Proverbs 11:12–21

What I Want to Remember . . .

_____

_____

_____

_____

———— ✓ ————

*There is in Jeremiah a strange mixture of toughness and tenderness.
There is warmth of spirit that is very sensitive to people's needs and to
God, and at the same time, there is steel-hard, bronze-like determina-
tion to stand firm against the tide of his times.*

—*Charles R. Swindoll*

Taken Captive by a Captive

Judah's sin had gone on long enough.

Hundreds of years had passed while king after king led God's people toward idolatrous and insincere worship. God's chosen people largely followed suit. They worshiped false gods. They thought only of their own interests. And they ignored God's prophets.

Jeremiah, God's prophet in the years leading up and into the exile of Judah, preached a message of judgment and restoration that fell on deaf ears. With Jerusalem under siege from the powerful Babylonian army, the king of Judah, Zedekiah, decided to hold Jeremiah captive so the prophet would not discourage the people with his message of doom (Jeremiah 32:3). Jeremiah was, at that moment, the captive of a captive. He sat trapped in the palace, surrounded by the king's guard. King Zedekiah's plight paralleled that of the prophet — the king sat trapped in his capital city, surrounded by an army from which he could not escape.

Even before his capture, Jeremiah was aware of the danger of speaking out. But instead of fleeing from his faulty leader, Jeremiah recognized the call of God on his life. He didn't run. But he didn't stay silent either. He spoke God's truth into the situation, even as a captive in the king's palace (32:2, 28).

No matter the danger, Jeremiah knew that God had called him to speak the truth to God's people. And he never stopped.

Week 42

Monday: Messages to the Kings
- ☐ Jeremiah 34–36
- ☐ Proverbs 11:22–31

Tuesday: Prison Time for Jeremiah
- ☐ Jeremiah 37–39
- ☐ Proverbs 12:1–10

Wednesday: A Nation in Turmoil
- ☐ Jeremiah 40–42
- ☐ Proverbs 12:11–19

Thursday: Cause and Effect
- ☐ Jeremiah 43–45
- ☐ Proverbs 12:20–28

Friday: More Bad News
- ☐ Jeremiah 46–48
- ☐ Proverbs 13:1–12

What I Want to Remember . . .

_____

_____

_____

_____

The Bible says little about your success but a lot about your heart. It is there that your character is formed and where true success is measured. Your heart's treasures are priceless—but they can be stolen. Are you guarding your heart?

—Charles R. Swindoll

How Life Works

Wisdom is not a list of dos and don'ts. The book of Proverbs may initially feel like a long catalog of one-liners on a variety of topics, but give them some extra thought and you'll discover that every wise statement is ultimately tied to God.

Rather than hard-and-fast rules, Proverbs offers godly principles best taught in the routines of life rather than a classroom.

Proverbs takes time. Unlike other books, Proverbs shouldn't be read in one sitting. Savor a few verses at a time and ponder the godly principle in play. Better yet, read one chapter of Proverbs each day for a month and you'll cover the whole book.

As you read Proverbs this week, consider how you would be wise to apply God's principles to your . . .

. . . *Generosity*: "One man gives freely, yet gains even more; another withholds unduly, but comes to poverty" (Proverbs 11:24 NIV).

. . . *Decision-making*: "The way of a fool seems right to him, but a wise man listens to advice" (12:15 NIV).

. . . *Conversation*: "Reckless words pierce like a sword, but the tongue of the wise brings healing" (12:18 NIV).

. . . *Other?*

Proverbs explains how life works. Although God isn't mentioned a great deal, take the book as a whole and learn how to be a wise follower of God's Word and God's ways.

Week 43

Monday: Let the Nations Fear the God of Israel
- [ ] Jeremiah 49–50
- [ ] Proverbs 13:13–25

Tuesday: Let Even Babylon Fear the God of Israel
- [ ] Jeremiah 51–52
- [ ] Proverbs 14:1–11

Wednesday: Disaster! God Judges the Sins of Jerusalem!
- [ ] Lamentations 1–2
- [ ] Proverbs 14:12–22

Thursday: Despair! Will God Remember Mercy?
- [ ] Lamentations 3–5
- [ ] Proverbs 14:23–35

Friday: Ezekiel's Commission: Boldly Speak God's Judgment
- [ ] Ezekiel 1–3
- [ ] Proverbs 15:1–11

What I Want to Remember . . .

_____

_____

_____

_____

It is God who makes evil result in sorrow, heartache, injustice, and despair. It is God's way of saying to us, "Now look, you must face the truth. You were made for Me. If you decide you don't want Me, then you will have to bear the consequences."

—*Charles R. Swindoll*

THE KEEPER OF PROMISES

We all know the benefits of keeping our word. If we say we will do something, we should do it.

That kind of follow-through is easy when it relates to rewarding good behavior. But it often feels like agony to follow through on the promise of discipline for bad behavior. Ask any parent.

God promised His people countless blessings in the Promised Land if they would follow Him. But if they chose to reject or ignore Him, God described the consequences in very clear terms.

The tragic book of Lamentations is Jeremiah's poignant reflection on the fact that God was simply following through on promises He made through Moses almost a thousand years before. God's response could easily have been the reward instead of the rod, but the nation had chosen to go its own way.

The Lord operates on similar terms today. God is still the Righteous Judge, the Keeper of Promises. Those who choose to reject or ignore Him will meet the frightful consequences of their own decisions (Galatians 5:7–8). Those who choose to follow Him will be blessed—for God "is a rewarder of those who seek Him" (Hebrews 11:6).

The choice is ours.

Week 44

Monday: Ezekiel Acts Out Jerusalem's Siege
- [ ] *Ezekiel 4–6*
- [ ] *Proverbs 15:12–22*

Tuesday: God's House Vandalized
- [ ] *Ezekiel 7–9*
- [ ] *Proverbs 15:23–33*

Wednesday: The Glory of God Leaves Town
- [ ] *Ezekiel 10–12*
- [ ] *Proverbs 16:1–11*

Thursday: Liars, Leaders, and Limbs . . . Consumed!
- [ ] *Ezekiel 13–15*
- [ ] *Proverbs 16:12–22*

Friday: God's Gracious Plan for Adulterous Jerusalem
- [ ] *Ezekiel 16–17*
- [ ] *Proverbs 16:23–33*

What I Want to Remember . . .

_____

_____

_____

_____

_____

God wanted to reveal His person and His glory to these captives through His prophet, Ezekiel. He wants to do that through us today. That's the analogy.

—*Charles R. Swindoll*

CENTER OF THE NATIONS

For thousands of years, the land of Israel sat in a strategic position as the only intercontinental land bridge between the superpowers of the ancient world. Therefore, any nation coming to or from Egypt—or traveling from the Mediterranean Sea to the Gulf of Aqaba—had to go through Israel. For years, Israel remained the crossroads for international imperialism, war, and trade.

This was no coincidence.

God intended Israel—as a kingdom of priests—to take a mediatory role among the nations. When world powers traveled through the land, God's people would either *influence* them for the Lord . . . or *be influenced* by them toward idolatry. Thus, Israel's central position among the nations proved to be a double-edged sword.

Ezekiel records God's lament that Jerusalem's placement "at the center of the nations" had borne no obedient fruit (Ezekiel 5:5–6). Instead, God's people had been swayed by the very nations God intended them to influence.

God has placed each of us where we live, work, and worship in order for us to influence others for His glory. As God appointed Ezekiel a "watchman to the house of Israel" (3:17), so the Lord calls us to share God's Word with those He brings to us . . . and those to whom He takes us (Colossians 4:6).

God calls us to make disciples of the nations rather than to become disciples of the nations.[13]

Week 45

Monday: God Desires Repentance
- ☐ Ezekiel 18–19
- ☐ Proverbs 17:1–14

Tuesday: Judgment Precedes Restoration
- ☐ Ezekiel 20–21
- ☐ Proverbs 17:15–28

Wednesday: The Destructive Power of Sin
- ☐ Ezekiel 22–24
- ☐ Proverbs 18:1–12

Thursday: The Lord Judges the Wicked
- ☐ Ezekiel 25–27
- ☐ Proverbs 18:13–24

Friday: Pride Leads to a Fall
- ☐ Ezekiel 28–30
- ☐ Proverbs 19:1–10

What I Want to Remember . . .

_____

_____

_____

_____

_____

God often asks His people to model His message. You can talk all day about God's sufficiency, but when the bottom drops out of your life and you model His sufficiency, that gets people's attention.

—*Charles R. Swindoll*

SUFFERING FOR A SIGN

Sometimes, God's ways just don't make sense.

As a spokesman for God, Ezekiel seemed to have it all—what better life could one hope for than experiencing direct communication from God and passing it on for the benefit of the people? But although Ezekiel was humbled and honored to speak God's word to the people, he suffered under the reality that those same people would not listen to his words.

Ezekiel's suffering reached its zenith when God informed the prophet that his wife would soon die (Ezekiel 24:15–18). And for what reason? So that an evil people could receive yet another warning of impending doom. Ezekiel knew that following after God would require him to suffer, but he never could have imagined this—that God would take the life of a good and faithful person in an attempt to save many. It made no sense to him.

How often we think the same. Except that God has done just that in Jesus.

In the aftermath of Jesus's sacrifice, the God of heaven and earth sometimes requires His people to suffer so that the many might have one more opportunity to be saved. Is such suffering easy or desirable? Of course not. But is it worth it? Absolutely. In the words of Jesus, "Not My will, but Yours be done" (Luke 22:42).

Week 46

Monday: Ezekiel: God's Watchman over Israel
- ☐ Ezekiel 31–33
- ☐ Proverbs 19:11–20

Tuesday: The Good Shepherd Cares for His Sheep
- ☐ Ezekiel 34–36
- ☐ Proverbs 19:21–29

Wednesday: The Haunting Valley of Dry Bones
- ☐ Ezekiel 37–39
- ☐ Proverbs 20:1–10

Thursday: Visions of the New Temple
- ☐ Ezekiel 40–42
- ☐ Proverbs 20:11–20

Friday: The Glory of God Returns to the Temple
- ☐ Ezekiel 43–45
- ☐ Proverbs 20:21–30

What I Want to Remember . . .

_____

_____

_____

_____

_____

When God's Word says something you don't like, beware of the temptation to alter your theology instead of adjusting your life.

—Charles R. Swindoll

Hope to Go On

Through Ezekiel, God wanted to reveal Himself to the Jews who were held captive in Babylon. It's easy to miss some subtleties in the book of Ezekiel, but please don't miss this point: God wanted to reveal His person and His glory to the exiles through His prophet Ezekiel.

Unless the captives in Babylon saw the glory of their majestic, all-powerful God, they would never regain their hope. The unmistakable message of Ezekiel's life is this: there is hope when you focus on God's glory. That is the full message God wanted to speak through Ezekiel.

The exiles who gathered by the rivers of Babylon had no earthly reason to smile. They had no song to sing. As they looked around, they saw an absence of anything that would revive their hope . . . but when they observed Ezekiel's dramatic object lessons and heard his message, they were reminded: God is alive. God is at work. His glory is here, in spite of our circumstances. That fact alone gave them reason to go on.

As God did with Ezekiel, so He wants to reveal His person and His glory through modern-day believers, as we have opportunities each day to reflect the light of His glory to all we meet.

Week 47

Monday: A Dead Sea Made Alive
- ☐ Ezekiel 46–48
- ☐ Proverbs 21:1–10

Tuesday: Testing Time at Babylon U
- ☐ Daniel 1–2
- ☐ Proverbs 21:11–20

Wednesday: To Bow or to Burn and the Felling of a Mighty Tree
- ☐ Daniel 3–4
- ☐ Proverbs 21:21–31

Thursday: The Finger of God and History, Prewritten
- ☐ Daniel 5–7
- ☐ Proverbs 22:1–10

Friday: The Judgment of the Dead and Learning How to Add
- ☐ Daniel 8–10
- ☐ Proverbs 22:11–21

What I Want to Remember . . .

_____

_____

_____

_____

Daniel was a man of the finest kind of strength. He was a man of absolute integrity—a sterling, unique illustration of God's presence. I'd like people to say the same thing about your life and mine.

—Charles R. Swindoll

True Patriotism

It's a sure sign of decline when nations drift from the faith that helped establish them. No nation testifies to this truth more than the nation of Israel.

Profane and foolish, the once-great kingdom was divided in two and conquered by foreign powers. In 605 BC, the southern kingdom, known as Judah, had some of its citizens taken away by the Babylonian armies. One man caught in that flood was Daniel.

Almost seventy years after Daniel's deportation, he read a portion of the scroll of Jeremiah pertaining to the length of the Jews' exile in Babylon (Daniel 9; Jeremiah 25:8–12). Realizing that this prophecy was on the eve of fulfillment, Daniel dropped to his knees in prayer for his forsaken country. Daniel confessed his nation's sins and affirmed God's character (Daniel 9:4–14). And he pleaded that God would hear, forgive, and take action to restore the temple and the nation to its former glory (9:15–19).

Daniel lived during trying times, and so do we. From his knees, Daniel shows us that a true patriot is one who prays earnestly for his or her country. The most noble acts of patriotism do not occur when we stand during our country's national anthem but when we kneel before the One who creates nations and destroys them.[14]

Week 48

Monday: Wars of the Greeks and Tribulations to Come
- ☐ *Daniel 11–12*
- ☐ *Proverbs 22:22–29*

Tuesday: Eventual Restoration Promised to Unfaithful Israel
- ☐ *Hosea 1–3*
- ☐ *Proverbs 23:1–9*

Wednesday: God Opens His Dispute with Unfaithful Israel
- ☐ *Hosea 4–6*
- ☐ *Proverbs 23:10–21*

Thursday: God Presents His Evidence against Unfaithful Israel
- ☐ *Hosea 7–9*
- ☐ *Proverbs 23:22–35*

Friday: God Regretfully Passes Judgment, yet Promises Eventual Restoration
- ☐ *Hosea 10–12*
- ☐ *Proverbs 24:1–12*

What I Want to Remember . . .

Paul, being a Jew, was very concerned that the Jews who read his letter to the Romans understood they had not been set aside forever—that the blindness that had come over them was not a permanent blindness, that there was and is a future.

—Charles R. Swindoll

ONE KING, ONE KINGDOM

Around 750 BC, Hosea was ordained to be a symbol of God's relationship with Israel. His commission involved taking an unfaithful wife and fathering three children by her. The children's names were symbolic, and the third child was called "Lo-ammi," which means "not my people." God was preparing to disown Israel.

But Hosea's redemption of his wayward wife symbolized a future hope of reconciliation between God and the spiritually rebellious northern tribes. For a season, they would have no king and would flounder in their worship. But "in the last days"—a day yet future—they will be restored, united again under a Davidic king and in proper relationship with the Lord (Hosea 3:4–5).

Hosea revealed, however, that before those last days, there would be judgment for their unfaithfulness. And God presented irrefutable evidence against them. God is gracious and long-suffering, but He also keeps His word. Hosea predicted that a time would soon come when the guilty would hear their verdict (Exodus 34:7). And being "sons of Israel" would not bring them immunity from sin's consequences.

Today, we remember that our own wanton rebellion has been dealt with through faith in Christ, and in Him we face no condemnation (Romans 8:1). Hosea reminds us that "in the last days," Israel's remnant will repent and claim Jesus Christ as Messiah. At that time, believers of all generations will be united under Him in right relationship with God.

Week 49

Monday: From Destruction Blossoms Blessing
- ☐ Hosea 13–14
- ☐ Proverbs 24:13–22

Tuesday: God Uses Calamity to Get the Attention of His People
- ☐ Joel 1–3
- ☐ Proverbs 24:23–34

Wednesday: All Humanity Is Guilty before God
- ☐ Amos 1–3
- ☐ Proverbs 25:1–10

Thursday: The Easy Life: Walking Far from God
- ☐ Amos 4–6
- ☐ Proverbs 25:11–20

Friday: Judgment Comes for the Wicked
- ☐ Amos 7–9
- ☐ Proverbs 25:21–28

What I Want to Remember . . .

_____

_____

_____

_____

———— ✓ ————

God has chosen plain, ordinary Amos-type folks to do His work. Take a long look at your short life and ask yourself, "Am I really on target?" If you're just the ordinary type of individual who by the grace of God has been picked up by the neck and pushed to a place to be used—be used. Let it happen.

—Charles R. Swindoll

BEWARE THE COMFORTABLE

Amos is among the chief biblical representatives of what we might call "the little people." A simple fig farmer from the village of Tekoa, Amos had no pretentiousness about him. He wasn't royalty. He exhibited no evidence of excessive riches. And he lived outside the great cultural centers of Israel and Judah.

Through Amos, God spoke most of His prophecies against the northern kingdom of Israel. Amos lived during a time of great material prosperity in Israel. However, as the people's material wealth and overall comfort increased, their moral values decreased, leaving the nation closer than ever to destruction.

Seeing the people's attitude in the midst of their material pleasures, Amos called out warnings. He pronounced woe on "those who [were] at ease in Zion," warned of exile to "those who recline[d] on beds of ivory," and decried that Israel had turned "justice into poison" (Amos 6:1, 4, 12). More than ever, the people's comfort had blinded them to their disobedience of God. They looked around and believed God had blessed them. But the truth was that their hearts—and therefore, their lives—were far from Him (3:6–8, 12; 4:9; 8:4).

The self-serving pleasures of life in a prosperous country had led the people away from God. Only by finding pleasure in the service of God and others would they ever find the eternal comfort we all seek.

Week 50

Monday: The Tale of Two Mountains
- [ ] *Obadiah*
- [ ] *Proverbs 26:1–14*

Tuesday: A Whale of a Tale
- [ ] *Jonah 1–4*
- [ ] *Proverbs 26:15–28*

Wednesday: Listen Up: The Lord Is Not Happy with You
- [ ] *Micah 1–3*
- [ ] *Proverbs 27:1–13*

Thursday: Listen Up: The Lord Will Bring Forth a Prince of Peace
- [ ] *Micah 4–5*
- [ ] *Proverbs 27:14–27*

Friday: Listen Up: The Lord Has Shown You What Is Good
- [ ] *Micah 6–7*
- [ ] *Proverbs 28:1–14*

What I Want to Remember . . .

_____

_____

_____

_____

_____

If you are proud and find pleasure in another's calamity, your success will soon diminish.

—Charles R. Swindoll

Humiliating the Haughty

Esau was the embodiment of this proverb:

> Pride goes before destruction,
> And a haughty spirit before stumbling.
> (Proverbs 16:18)

So selfishly proud was Esau, the twin brother of Jacob, that this character trait seemed to pass through his DNA to his children and his children's children, the Edomites. During an ongoing family feud with Judah (the descendents of Jacob), the people of Edom sat proudly in their mountainous hideout and gloated over the troubles that had befallen Judah. Not only did the Edomites refuse to help their brothers who had fled from Jerusalem, they even killed some of them (Obadiah 1:10–12).

For such pride, God sent the prophet Obadiah to pronounce judgment against Edom. God would restore Judah and use the descendants of Jacob as a punishing rod against Edom, driving them from their lofty perch.

Obadiah's prophecy came to pass—Edom fell and is no more. Esau and his descendants had no need for God; they thought they had their stronghold to protect them and their wise men to guide them. So profane was Esau that he is called "godless" in Hebrews 12:16. And so he was. And so are all of us who strut through life as though God does not sit on high condemning the proud and commending the humble.

We must never forget the lesson of Edom taught through the pen of Obadiah: God honors the humble and humiliates the haughty.

Week 51

Monday: Warning to Nineveh
- ☐ Nahum 1–3
- ☐ Proverbs 28:15–28

Tuesday: How to Complain to God
- ☐ Habakkuk 1–3
- ☐ Proverbs 29:1–9

Wednesday: Woes and Worship
- ☐ Zephaniah 1–3
- ☐ Proverbs 29:10–18

Thursday: Wake Up, Israel!
- ☐ Haggai 1–2
- ☐ Proverbs 29:19–27

Friday: The Right Word at the Right Time
- ☐ Zechariah 1–3
- ☐ Proverbs 30:1–10

What I Want to Remember . . .

_____

_____

_____

_____

_____

You are perhaps most effective in your life when you make a determinative effort to stop and rest in God. Stop resisting. Stop complaining. Stop the fighting. Just wait and see what God does.

—Charles R. Swindoll

Faith in the Midst of a Tornado

Anyone who has suffered injustice will have a heart for Habakkuk. This desperate, sometimes angry prophet saw tragedy heading his way like a tornado, but he couldn't get out of its path. Even harder to accept was the fact that God had custom-designed the impending storm . . . by the hand of Israel's most ruthless enemy, the Babylonians.

How could God allow this? Was this fair?

Nothing short of captivity would get Israel's attention. Habakkuk could not argue that Israel deserved discipline; his issue was with God's method of using the Babylonians, a godless, evil people.

Confused, Habakkuk didn't know how to pray. So he made the most significant decision of his life: he stopped wrestling with the seeming injustice and, instead, stood back to wait and watch. He let God's timing run its course.

And then God showed up. He described for Habakkuk a vision that spelled out the Babylonians' certain destruction. He assured Habakkuk that He would not forget Israel. And He reminded Habakkuk to trust Him, regardless of present circumstances.

Habakkuk responded with a confidence in God that trumped his inability to fully understand all that was happening. Israel's situation still looked bad, but now Habakkuk knew for certain that God was good . . . and that God was God. For Habakkuk, that was enough.

Week 52

Monday: Light, Trees, Scrolls, and Chariots
- ☐ Zechariah 4–6
- ☐ Proverbs 30:11–23

Tuesday: Softening Hard Hearts . . . and the Coming King
- ☐ Zechariah 7–9
- ☐ Proverbs 30:24–33

Wednesday: In That Day . . . Looking toward Armageddon
- ☐ Zechariah 10–12
- ☐ Proverbs 31:1–9

Thursday: The Coming(s) of Christ Predicted
- ☐ Zechariah 13–14
- ☐ Proverbs 31:10–20

Friday: A Book for the Backsliders
- ☐ Malachi 1–4
- ☐ Proverbs 31:21–31

What I Want to Remember . . .

_____

_____

_____

Malachi prophesied of the Messiah and His forerunner. And then there was silence—for four centuries. The next voice from God is one crying in the wilderness—the Baptizer, the forerunner announcing the Messiah. You who are waiting on God, take heart! God doesn't forget His own. He will shine His sun of righteousness in your life, in His good time.

—Charles R. Swindoll

LOOKING FOR HIS COMING

The modern-day slope of the Mount of Olives has a sign that claims the location of the prophet Zechariah's tomb. The prophet foresaw Israel's King coming on a donkey, and that's exactly how Jesus presented Himself as He rode down the Mount of Olives at His triumphal entry (Zechariah 9:9, 16; Matthew 21:5). How ironic that Zechariah would allegedly rest on the very slope where his words found fulfillment.

Today, the steep slope follows a narrow road with high walls on either side. The southern wall overlooks a vast Jewish graveyard. Thousands of white tombs give testimony to the hope that when Messiah comes, "His feet will stand on the Mount of Olives" (Zechariah 14:4); the assumption is that those buried there will receive special blessings. Although the Messiah *will* raise all Jews from these graves, sadly, not every resurrection will result in reward (Daniel 12:2; Revelation 20:11–15).

On the other side of the road, the high wall to the north encloses the grounds of the Dominus Flevit Church. The chapel and its Latin name memorialize the moment on the donkey when "the Lord wept" over Jerusalem because His people would reject Him (Luke 19:41–42).

These two walls offer a startling contrast. One wall guards the hope that the Messiah *will come* one day. The other wall guards the belief that He *already has come*—but was rejected.

Only a narrow, steep road separates these two walls . . . but the distance between them is eternal.[15]

How to Begin a Relationship with God

The Old Testament bears witness to the basic pieces of God's redemptive plan for humanity: creation, fall, and re-creation. God created man and woman in the garden of Eden. However, the man and woman sinned, disobeying God's simple command to not eat from the tree of the knowledge of good and evil. That sin resulted in separation from God and the need for redemption and re-creation, which would come in the person of the promised Messiah.

The New Testament goes on to reveal the identity of the Messiah—our Savior—Jesus, God's own Son. But how can we receive the salvation and new life He offers? How can we have a relationship with Jesus? The Bible marks the path with four essential truths. Let's look at each marker in detail.

Our Spiritual Condition: Totally Depraved

The first truth is rather personal. One look in the mirror of Scripture, and our human condition becomes painfully clear:

> "There is none righteous, not even one;
> There is none who understands,
> There is none who seeks for God;
> All have turned aside, together they have
>   become useless;
> There is none who does good,
> There is not even one." (Romans 3:10–12)

We are all sinners through and through—totally depraved. Now, that doesn't mean we've committed every atrocity known to humankind. We're not as *bad* as we can be, just as *bad off* as we can be. Sin colors all our thoughts, motives, words, and actions.

If you've been around a while, you likely already believe it. Look around. Everything around us bears the smudge marks of our sinful nature. Despite our best efforts to create a perfect world, crime statistics continue to soar, divorce rates keep climbing, and families keep crumbling.

Something has gone terribly wrong in our society and in ourselves—something deadly. Contrary to how the world would repackage it, "me-first" living doesn't equal rugged individuality and freedom; it equals death. As Paul said in his letter to the Romans, "The wages of sin is death" (Romans 6:23)—our spiritual and physical death that comes from God's righteous judgment of our sin, along with all of the emotional and practical effects of this separation that we experience on a daily basis. This brings us to the second marker: God's character.

God's Character: Infinitely Holy

How can God judge us for a sinful state we were born into? Our total depravity is only half the answer. The other half is God's infinite holiness.

The fact that we know things are not as they should be points us to a standard of goodness beyond ourselves. Our sense of injustice in life on this side of eternity implies a perfect standard of justice beyond our reality. That standard and source is God Himself. And God's standard of holiness contrasts starkly with our sinful condition.

Scripture says that "God is Light, and in Him there is no darkness at all" (1 John 1:5). God is absolutely holy—which creates a problem for us. If He is so pure, how can we who are so impure relate to Him?

Perhaps we could try being better people, try to tilt the balance in favor of our good deeds, or seek out methods for self-improvement. Throughout history, people have attempted to live up to God's standard by keeping the Ten Commandments or living by their own code of ethics. Unfortunately, no one can come close to satisfying the demands of God's law. Romans 3:20 says, "By the works of the Law no flesh will be justified in His sight; for through the Law comes the knowledge of sin."

Our Need: A Substitute

So here we are, sinners by nature and sinners by choice, trying to pull ourselves up by our own bootstraps to attain a relationship with our holy Creator. But every time we try, we fall flat on our faces. We can't live a good enough life to make up for our sin, because God's standard isn't "good enough"—it's *perfection*. And we can't make amends for the offense our sin has created without dying for it.

Who can get us out of this mess?

If someone could live perfectly, honoring God's law, and would bear sin's death penalty for us—in our place—then we would be saved from our predicament. But is there such a person? Thankfully, yes!

Meet your substitute—*Jesus Christ*. He is the One who took death's place for you!

> [God] made [Jesus Christ] who knew no
> sin to be sin on our behalf, so that we might
> become the righteousness of God in Him.
> (2 Corinthians 5:21)

God's Provision: A Savior

God rescued us by sending His Son, Jesus, to die on the cross for our sins (1 John 4:9–10). Jesus was fully human and fully divine (John 1:1, 18), a truth that ensures His understanding of our weaknesses, His power to forgive, and His ability to bridge the gap between God and us (Romans 5:6–11). In short, we are "justified as a gift by His grace through the redemption which is in Christ Jesus" (Romans 3:24). Two words in this verse bear further explanation: *justified* and *redemption*.

Justification is God's act of mercy, in which He declares righteous the believing sinners while we are still in our sinning state. Justification doesn't mean that God *makes* us righteous, so that we never sin again, rather that He *declares* us righteous—much like a judge pardons a guilty criminal. Because Jesus took our sin upon Himself and suffered our judgment on the cross, God forgives our debt and proclaims us PARDONED.

Redemption is Christ's act of paying the complete price to release us from sin's bondage. God sent His Son to bear His wrath for all of our sins—past, present, and future (Romans 3:24–26; 2 Corinthians 5:21). In humble obedience, Christ willingly endured the shame of the cross for our sake (Mark 10:45; Romans 5:6–8; Philippians 2:8). Christ's death satisfied God's righteous demands. He no longer holds our sins against us, because His own Son paid the penalty for them. We are freed from the slave market of sin, never to be enslaved again!

Placing Your Faith in Christ

These four truths describe how God has provided a way to Himself through Jesus Christ. Because the price has been paid in full by God, we must respond to His free gift of eternal life in total faith and confidence in Him to save us. We must step forward into the relationship with God that He has prepared for us—not by doing good works or by being a good person, but by coming to Him just as we are and accepting His justification and redemption by faith.

> For by grace you have been saved through faith; and that not of yourselves, it is the gift of God; not as a result of works, so that no one may boast. (Ephesians 2:8–9)

We accept God's gift of salvation simply by placing our faith in Christ alone for the forgiveness of our sins. Would you like to enter a relationship with your Creator by trusting in Christ as your Savior? If so, here's a simple prayer you can use to express your faith:

> *Dear God,*
>
> *I know that my sin has put a barrier between You and me. Thank You for sending Your Son, Jesus, to die in my place. I trust in Jesus alone to forgive my sins, and I accept His gift of eternal life. I ask Jesus to be my personal Savior and the Lord of my life. Thank You. In Jesus's name, amen.*

If you've prayed this prayer or one like it and you wish to find out more about knowing God and His plan for you in the Bible, contact us at Insight for Living. Our contact information is on the following pages.

WE ARE HERE FOR YOU

If you desire to find out more about knowing God and His plan for you in the Bible, contact us. Insight for Living provides staff pastors who are available for free written correspondence or phone consultation. These seminary-trained and seasoned counselors have years of experience and are well-qualified guides for your spiritual journey.

Please feel welcome to contact your regional Pastoral Ministries by using the information below:

United States
Insight for Living
Pastoral Ministries
Post Office Box 269000
Plano, Texas 75026-9000
USA
972-473-5097, Monday through Friday,
8:00 a.m.–5:00 p.m. central time
www.insight.org/contactapastor

Canada
Insight for Living Canada
Pastoral Ministries
PO Box 8 Stn A
Abbotsford BC V2T 6Z4
CANADA
1-800-663-7639
info@insightforliving.ca

Australia, New Zealand, and South Pacific

Insight for Living Australia
Pastoral Care
Post Office Box 443
Boronia, VIC 3155
AUSTRALIA
1300 467 444

United Kingdom and Europe

Insight for Living United Kingdom
Pastoral Care
PO Box 553
Dorking
RH4 9EU
UNITED KINGDOM
0800 787 9364
+44 (0)1306 640156
pastoralcare@insightforliving.org.uk

Endnotes

1. Adapted from Wayne Stiles, *Going Places with God: A Devotional Journey through the Lands of the Bible* (Ventura, Calif.: Regal, 2006), 60. Used by permission.

2. Adapted from Stiles, *Going Places with God*, 139.

3. Adapted from Stiles, *Going Places with God*, 73.

4. Adapted from Stiles, *Going Places with God*, 103.

5. Taken from Wayne Stiles, "Unwise Cracks," *Insights* (Insight for Living, Sept. 2005): 1–2.

6. Adapted from Stiles, *Going Places with God*, 136.

7. Adapted from Stiles, *Going Places with God*, 107.

8. Adapted from Stiles, *Going Places with God*, 69.

9. Adapted from Stiles, *Going Places with God*, 138.

10. Adapted from Stiles, *Going Places with God*, 117.

11. Adapted from Stiles, *Going Places with God*, 123.

12. Adapted from Stiles, *Going Places with God*, 74.

13. Adapted from Stiles, *Going Places with God*, 124.

14. Adapted from the message, "True Patriotism: Praying for Your Nation," from the series *No Doubt: Godlessness become Godliness, A Study of the Book of Daniel* by Derrick G. Jeter, Coffee House Fellowship, Stonebriar Community Church, Frisco, Texas, May 17, 2009. Copyright © 2009 by Derrick G. Jeter. Used by permission. All rights reserved worldwide.

15. Adapted from Wayne Stiles, *Walking in the Footsteps of Jesus: A Journey Through the Lands and Lessons of Christ* (Ventura, Calif.: Regal, 2008), 114–16. Used by permission.

Resources for Probing Further

To further your study of the Old Testament, we recommend the following resources. Of course, we cannot always endorse everything a writer or ministry says, so we encourage you to approach these and all other non-biblical resources with wisdom and discernment.

Barker, Kenneth L., and John R. Kohlenberger III, eds. *The Expositor's Bible Commentary: Old Testament*. Abridged ed. Grand Rapids: Zondervan, 2004.

Beitzel, Barry J. *The New Moody Atlas of the Bible*. Chicago: Moody Press, 2009.

Chisholm, Robert B., Jr. *Interpreting the Minor Prophets*. Grand Rapids: Zondervan, 1990.

Dyer, Charles, and Gene Merrill. *The Old Testament Explorer: Discovering the Essence, Background, and Meaning of Every Book in the Old Testament*. Nashville: Thomas Nelson, 2001.

Jensen, Irving. *Jensen's Survey of the Old Testament*. Chicago: Moody Publishers, 1978.

Merrill, Eugene H. *Kingdom of Priests: A History of Old Testament Israel*. 2nd ed. Grand Rapids: Baker Academic, 2008.

Radmacher, Earl D., Ronald B. Allen, and H. W. House, eds. *Nelson's New Illustrated Bible Commentary: Spreading the Light of God's Word into Your Life*. Nashville: Thomas Nelson, 1999.

Tenney, Merrill C., ed. *Zondervan's Pictorial Bible Dictionary*. Grand Rapids: Zondervan, 1999.

Walton, John H. *Chronological and Background Charts of the Old Testament*. Rev. ed. Grand Rapids: Zondervan, 1994.

Walvoord, John F., and Roy B. Zuck, eds. *The Bible Knowledge Commentary: Old Testament*. Wheaton, Ill.: Victor Books, 1985.

Wiersbe, Warren W. *The Wiersbe Bible Commentary: Old Testament*. Colorado Springs: David C. Cook, 2007.

Yancey, Philip. *The Bible Jesus Read*. Grand Rapids: Zondervan, 1999.

ORDERING INFORMATION

If you would like to order additional copies of *Insight's Bible Reading Guide: Old Testament* or to order other Insight for Living resources, please contact the office that serves you.

United States
Insight for Living
Post Office Box 269000
Plano, Texas 75026-9000
USA
1-800-772-8888
(Monday through Friday, 7:00 a.m.–7:00 p.m. central time)
www.insight.org
www.insightworld.org

Canada
Insight for Living Canada
PO Box 8 Stn A
Abbotsford BC V2T 6Z4
CANADA
1-800-663-7639
www.insightforliving.ca

Australia, New Zealand, and South Pacific
Insight for Living Australia
Post Office Box 443
Boronia, VIC 3155
AUSTRALIA
1300 467 444
www.insight.asn.au

United Kingdom and Europe

Insight for Living United Kingdom
PO Box 553
Dorking
RH4 9EU
UNITED KINGDOM
0800 787 9364
www.insightforliving.org.uk

Other International Locations

International constituents may contact the U.S. office through our Web site (www.insightworld.org), mail queries, or by calling +1-972-473-5136.